D0068517

SPIRITUALITY FOR MINISTRY

Urban T. Holmes, III

Foreword by Loren B. Mead

MOREHOUSE PUBLISHING

Harrisburg, Pennsylvania

Morehouse Publishing
P.O. Box 1321
Harrisburg, PA 17105
Morehouse Publishing is a division of The Morehouse Group.

All Bible quotations, unless otherwise noted, are from the New English Bible.

Cover design by Corey Kent

Library of Congress Cataloging-in-Publication Data

Holmes, Urban Tigner, 1930-
  Spirituality for ministry / Urban T. Holmes III.
      p. cm.—(Library of Episcopalian classics)
Originally published: San Francisco : Harper & Row, 1982.
Includes index.
  ISBN 0-8192-1916-9 (pbk.)
  1. Clergy—Religious life. 2. Spirituality. I. Title. II. Series.
  BV4011.6 .H64 2002
  248.8'92—dc21

                                          2002006261

Printed in the United States of America

02 03 04 05 06 07 08 09   8 7 6 5 4 3 2 1

Contents

For My Teachers

Foreword

By Loren B. Mead
THE ALBAN INSTITUTE

WITH THIS book, the formal publications from the pen of Urban Tigner Holmes, III, clearly one of the most influential Episcopal thinkers, teachers, and theologians of the twentieth century, come to an end. On August 6, 1981, the Feast of the Transfiguration, the earthly pilgrimage of that remarkable priest came to an end. Yet Terry Holmes's major contributions to the life of his beloved Church are yet to come. Those contributions will be made through the minds he set on fire in the classroom and in the study, during conferences he led and in the extraordinary discussions that seemed to take place wherever he put his feet up on a coffee table, poured a long bourbon, and pushed his glasses up on his forehead.

This book was a labor of love during Terry's year of sabbatical from teaching and administration at the School of Theology of the University of the South in Sewanee, Tennessee. From Kanuga, the Episcopal conference center in Hendersonville, North Carolina, he crisscrossed the country, talking and listening. He talked less than he listened, however, because he was trying to learn from people who are not often listened to by teachers and administrators. Parish pastors were his teachers; it was their experience to which he was listening.

But it was not random listening he did. He had done his homework, read and ordered the questions, discovered the instrumentation by which to listen more creatively. This book is the result of that listening and of his ordering of what he heard.

There is much that is revolutionary in what he did, in what is included in this book. He talks about doing theology "from the ground up," and that is precisely what he works at here—going to the practitioners of parish ministry to hear what it is like to try to say your prayers there, to see how the ancient disciplines inform them or—and he has no difficulty thinking the unthinkable—how their experiences force reinterpretation of what the ancient disciplines have to say.

It is important, however, to make one real distinction. When Terry Holmes does theology from the ground up, it is on the basis of an enormous knowledge of the best the Church and its fathers and mothers have said and done through the two thousand years of the Church's history. It is also on the basis of the best scholarship available on what our Greek and Hebrew traditions bring to the Church's history and of the pressure of secular learning of our day. Terry's theology from the ground up is not a mindless, ahistorical ramble through witness, an off-the-cuff commentary masquerading as theology. He demanded vigor and depth of scholarly grounding, not chatter. He was passionate about that. But his passion demanded an equal portion of cool, precise, sometimes even objective thinking. As a matter of fact, I heard the Archbishop of Canterbury characterize Terry in a sermon, just a month after his death, as exemplifying "passionate coolness."

Passionate coolness did not mean clarity of manuscript, however! Terry, through his wife, Jane, asked me to work with his editors at Harper & Row to get the manuscript in shape for publication. In the course of working on it, I have once again been forced to come to grips with that marvelous intellect, that raucous sense of humor, and that towering personality that many of us came to depend on personally and professionally. I hope we have crossed his t's and dotted his i's adequately; but in terms of what this book is about, all we have been up to is picking fleas off an elephant.

This last book may be Terry's most revolutionary. Perhaps his last gift to us, his colleagues and his friends, will be the pressure within us to pursue the paths he has opened up, to explore the possibilities he has pointed us to. That would be no small gift.

Preface

THE OCCASION and means for the writing of this book were due to the gracious support of a number of people. Robert Ayres, Vice-Chancellor of the University of the South, made sure I took a sabbatical leave in the winter of 1980 and spring of 1981. The faculty of the School of Theology there did their best to see that the seminary functioned in my absence. The university gave me a research grant that, added to the generous support of a personal friend, made it possible for Jane and me to do the necessary thing: leave home for seven months.

Edgar Hartley, Director of the Kanuga Conference Center near Hendersonville, North Carolina, and the Reverend LaRue Downing, Program Director of Kanuga, created the post of theologian-in-residence just in time for me to be its first occupant. The very light duties assigned to me in that function and the supportive counsel of LaRue throughout its term added immeasurably to the experience out of which this book was written. The Reverend and Mrs. Robert L. Haden, Jr., provided their home near Kanuga for our residence, which could not have been more suited to our needs.

The Reverend Alexander Viola, Rector of St. James Church, Hendersonville, North Carolina, and the people of his parish welcomed us and gave me a particularly important gift during this time: the sense of being a priest within a community. Our friends in Hendersonville have become an important part of our lives. The Episcopal Diocese of Western North Carolina, of which I have been a priest for the past five years, did much to make us feel back at home.

I am particularly grateful to the clergy who constituted the research sample; they allowed me to come into their private lives, to poke and probe, and to ask the difficult question. They never failed to try to answer and were always good-natured about some sensitive areas of their lives. In a very real sense this book belongs to them.

How do I thank my secretary, Pat Smith, who served as a buffer between the seminary and me in western North Carolina; my typist, Lisa Kirby, who had to decipher all my changes; and Jane, who is always there?

This list of those who have made this book possible is very humbling. In dedicating it, though, I have sought to reach even beyond them and recognize those who as teachers contributed to my development as a theologian, without implying any fault in them for my deficiencies.

URBAN T. HOLMES
The Feast of the Venerable Bede, 1981

Introduction

A RETREAT master when I was a seminarian told us that if we were marooned on a desert island and could choose to have three books with us, we should choose the Bible, the *Book of Common Prayer* (an obvious choice for Episcopal seminarians), and Frederic P. Harton's *Elements of the Spiritual Life*. Harton's book is one of those products of Anglo-Catholic scholarship that flourished between the two world wars and consists of a totally nondiscriminating assimilation and regurgitation for unsuspecting Anglicans of the worst in post-Vatican I Roman Catholic theology. I do not believe I ever knew more than one or two persons who read it all the way through, although it undoubtedly gathers dust on the shelves of many an Anglican priest's study. History had progressed and left behind the world for which the ideas in this book were relevant before Harton—may his intention be blessed!—ever put pen to paper.

Probably every denomination has its own *Elements of the Spiritual Life*. I was also required to labor through parts of Adolphe Tanquerey's *The Spiritual Life*, which is a Roman Catholic version of Harton's book. In the research for this present study I found mention of other, similar books. They all seem to occupy that corner of our library where we keep books containing thoughts of the past for which we have nostalgic reverence even though we admit, sometimes only privately, that they bear no discernable relation to the life we live today.

But the intentions of authors such as Harton cannot be faulted. He wished to help us develop a prayer life that expresses an awareness of God's presence in our everyday lives. The problem lay in the execution of that intention. On the one hand, he was closely tied to a tradition that appeared limited by time and geography. On the other hand, as far as we can tell he ignored what was happening in the world in which he lived and consequently wrote for a church people who lived largely in his fantasies. Far too much spiritual theology suffers from such limited insight, despite its very laudable intentions.

In the writing of this book I too share the desire of those who have gone before for a holy clergy and a church that prays. But I want to avoid as carefully as possible defining too closely what the shape of prayer, clerical or lay, should be today. Any understanding of contemporary spirituality has to come from combining an interpretation of the tradition that is as wide as possible with a comprehension of the signs of our times. To this end I have done several things in preparation for writing this book on spirituality and the clergy.

First, I have listened to learn what they believe the spiritual life is today and how they practice it. This listening has taken a number of forms, beginning with my daily contacts with fellow priests and pastors. Chance meetings, periodic conversations, and occasional seminars have provided me both prior to writing and during the months spent in composition with the opportunity to gather data informally.

More specifically for the purposes of this study, I wrote the judicatory heads of five denominations in the area where I was living during my work on this book and asked each of them to nominate five or six ordained persons whom they considered "spiritually mature." This is an ecumenical study, but certain logistic limits on the extent of the research were required. The denominations I contacted were the Roman Catholic, Episcopalian, Presbyterian, Lutheran (LCA), and United Methodist. Once I received the names of these persons, I wrote and asked them to participate in the study on a confidential basis in two ways.

Each participant was asked to complete a series of four psychological inventories: the Myers-Briggs Type Indicator, the World View Study, the Bem Sex Role Inventory, and my own, which I call the Spiritual Style Inventory. I do not believe it is possible to "measure" spirituality, but my hypothesis is that there are different personality profiles within the clergy and I wished to explore correlations between personality types, worldview, and the relationship of feminine to masculine consciousness with possible styles of spirituality, as well as to discern if any one personality pattern predominated. The Myers-Briggs is a well-known inventory of personality types based upon Jungian categories. The World View Study, prepared by James Hopewell of Emory University and his colleagues, operates on the theory that people look at their environment from predominantly one of four possible points of view described as canonic, empiric, gnostic, and charismatic. The Bem Sex Role Inventory, which is a measure of femininity and masculinity in relation to one another and to possible androgynous consciousness, was developed by Sandra L. Bem of Stanford University.

I myself have worked out an inventory that seeks to delineate styles of spirituality on the basis of two scales: apophatic/kataphatic and speculative/affective. The assumption that lies behind the first scale is that prayer tends to take the form either of an emptying of images (apophatic) or of the quest for vivid images (kataphatic). The assumption behind the second is that as we pray we encourage in ourselves either cognitive relationship to God (speculative) or an emotional relationship (affective).

In this study the use of the inventories has proved suggestive on occasion, and I have indicated where that is the case, but I must point out that they were not the sole or even primary basis for the research. The second phase of the work with the participants, a taped interview following a standard format, provided a relatively clear and consistent picture of the nature of the spiritual life within the sample.

In setting up the research, however, I did not find it possible to do everything as neatly as I had originally planned. As I expected, the method of selecting the sample was subject to a certain skewing by the bias of the judicatory heads,[1] although this proved not to be as big a factor as I feared. I found it impossible to get into the Methodist system in the manner I had hoped and I had to recruit Methodist participants on my own. No blacks or women were nominated, a problem I was only able to remedy in regard to women clergy. Several of the persons suggested to me declined to participate on grounds ranging from lack of time to theological objection to the study. And there is not a complete congruence between those doing the inventories and those interviewed—two who did the inventories I could not reach for interviews and five were interviewed who did not complete the inventories.

All in all, the research sample involved twenty-two persons: two women and twenty men. There were four Roman Catholics, eleven Episcopalians (five of whom did not complete inventories), three Lutherans, four Presbyterians, and two Methodists. In the book I only occasionally identify the denominational affiliation of the person I am citing, for the reason that in almost all instances it was found to be irrelevant. There simply were no radical deviations from the general

pattern of responses for this group on the basis of denomination. This
has led me to conclude that there is a common, generally tacit, emerging pattern of prayer for the clergy in the Christian denominations
that are heirs of the more classical Reformation of the sixteenth century (including here the Roman Catholic Reformation).

In an attempt to investigate and explain this pattern I was led in
two directions. One was to examine the tradition of Christian spirituality, to discern its meaning as best I could, and to place that beside
what seemed to be the present pattern of prayer. It was important to
get the full sweep of the last two thousand years, as well as to look at
both the Eastern and Western churches. As a basis for reflecting on the
tradition I used the work for my recent book *A History of Christian
Spirituality*.[2]

Obviously, however, the vast amount of material available from
the Christian spiritual masters cannot be fully assimilated by anyone
person. A certain selectivity is of necessity based on available time and
knowledge as well as personal bias. I have no desire to hide my particular outlook, and I want to be fair with the reader. Those spiritual
masters upon whom I particularly drew—Gregory of Nyssa, Richard
of St. Victor, Julian of Norwich, George Herbert, for example—are
persons whose writings illumine my thinking.

The other direction I took to explain what seems to be happening
among the clergy today was a phenomenological analysis of prayer in
our times. This is a more subtle exercise than the interpretation of the
tradition. As an anthropologist as well as a theologian, I have sought
to look at religion—particularly but not exclusively the Christian religion—in the late twentieth century as a participant-observer. I am
committed to the belief that with the prevailing anthropocentric
worldview, the only theology that can hope to be affirmed *au-
tonomously* by contemporary folk is one that begins where we are, a
theology done "from below." This includes spiritual theology as well as
dogmatic, moral, and pastoral theology. Certainly there are those today who preach something very different, the so-called creationists,
for example. In my judgment an approach like the one creationists
take is intellectual suicide and can only contribute to the future ex-
tinction of the Gospel among reasonable people.

To do theology from below it is necessary to discern what in contemporary meaning implies or points to the transcendent. I speak of
what Peter Berger some years ago discussed as a "rumor of angels" or
what others have called the "footprints of God." This attempt to find

the implications of current knowing for the presence of God is what foundational theology is all about. It would appear that at this time we have no single grand theory in foundational theology, but that we find in many areas potentially rich material. I have sought in this study to draw those areas, sometimes explicitly and sometimes only by implication, in order to ground contemporary clerical spirituality in a reasonable understanding of our world.

This book is not written just for the clergy. I am convinced of the validity of the concept that by virtue of our baptism all Christians are called to be ministers, a concept variously described as mutual ministry, total ministry, or shared ministry. Such a notion of ministry is a source of hope for the contemporary church, but mutual ministry is not a realistic possibility if we do not differentiate between the functions of the ordained and the lay. Without that explicit distinction, we find the movement frustrated for reasons that are not clearly understood. If we believe that all ministry is the same we are not looking at either the tradition or the present facts. We are embracing a false concept that makes those who disagree sound illiberal and has the effect of blocking a realistic reshaping of ministry today.

In this book I state my belief that the spirituality of clergy is *instrumentally* different than that of laity. This is obvious even in the lives of priests and pastors who vehemently deny there is any difference. But it is important that the whole church look at the spirituality of the clergy because of the ordained person's vocation to be an efficient cause of the deepened awareness of God in the life of the people of God. Therefore, my intended audience is the Christian community, the clergy and laity who wish to understand a point of view as to the life of prayer and the ordained person.

I. The Subject

1. The Spiritual Person

IT HAS been my experience that one does not drop the word "spiritual" into a conversation lightly. "How is your spiritual life?" I unwittingly asked a minister in the presence of some others. There was a sudden, discernable tension in the air, as if I had inquired into the intimate details of his sex life. Someone coughed and the person of whom I inquired, obviously sharing the embarrassment, felt he had to say something to me. After all, I was a fellow pastor. "Great," he said with an enthusiasm tinged with condescension. "I've really gotten it all together." Somehow "getting it together"—the tired jargon of humanistic psychology—was not what I had in mind, but now aware that I was treading on forbidden territory I let it pass.

Later on in a conversation with several of the same people, a colleague of mine who had the irritating habit of never rebuking me directly but always through intermediaries remarked, "Why are we asking people about their spiritual life?" Since I was the only one who asked, the "we" obviously meant me. "After all," he averred, "all of life is spiritual!" As I walked away somewhat chastened, I wondered why, if all of life is spiritual and my question had been pointless and unanswerable, the mention of the word so perceptibly heightened the anxiety of those gathered there.

This scenario has been repeated several times due to a stubborn streak that makes me keep asking questions in search of answers. After one such conversation I inquired of someone with whom I felt some rapport why the word "spiritual" evoked so much feeling. He replied, "I don't think we realized that you are charismatic. You know most of us have been pretty active in the civil rights movement and protesting the Vietnam War." I am not sure he spoke for anyone but

himself, but for him "spiritual" did not mean everything, "all of life";
it was something very specific. It was synonymous with "baptism in
the Holy Spirit," speaking in tongues, prayer meetings, and opposition
to the church's social action. It was the escape from the confrontations
of the 1960s. It was the enemy. I explained that I could hardly count
myself charismatic, and he looked puzzled. Obviously wishing to get
off the subject, he said, "Whatever it is, we don't do it."

I responded to his sensitivities, but something else came clear to
me at that moment. There is judgment connected with the word "spirituality," particularly when used by clergy of a certain generation. I remembered a classmate in seminary many years ago telling me why he
had transferred from another institution. In the former school during
his first year he had chosen a course entitled "The Life of Prayer." After three weeks of faithful attendance, he had not heard the word
"prayer" mentioned. That day after class he asked the instructor when
they would begin to discuss the subject of the course. With some anger
the instructor glared at this poor bumpkin. "Young man," he said, "a
hot bath will do you more good than all the prayer in the world."

Why the tension? Why the anxiety? Why the ferocity? Is it possible
that a whole generation of clergy rejected something they understood
to be spirituality, without totally removing from the conscience an inchoate, lingering suspicion that this is precisely what they are to be
about? Mention of spirituality provoked guilt, anger, and defensive-
ness in them.

Then came the renewed interest in spirituality in the church and
the tragedy was compounded. For almost a generation clergy have
pursued little classical education in spirituality and have had few
models for its practice. Caught in an enthusiasm that has touched the
lives of many church people, the word "spirituality" came to mean
whatever anyone wanted it to mean. Because of their ignorance—cul-
pable or not—there has been a serious lack among the church's leadership of the knowledge that gives substance and direction to a
contemporary form of the authentic spiritual renewal of the church.
Not infrequently they fall back on the worst kind of hick piety.

Devoid of clear meaning, spirituality has become a catchword for
whatever one favors or opposes. I have discovered that passing mention of spirituality can bring immediate acceptance by some or can
evoke intellectual skepticism in others. The cynicism of its detractors
is only reinforced.

In truth we use the word far too loosely. In my interviews with persons considered spirituality mature it was clare that there was no consensus as to what spirituality meant. "Spirituality" has too little intellectual substance. It has to be more than a name for warm feelings, which in our search for assurance we attribute to God. These feelings may very well be an intimation of our awareness of God's presence, but until we can distinguish spirituality from what it is not—an initial criterion for any definition—then we do not know what it is. It cannot be everything and have any meaning. The word needs to point to a discrete, identifiable something before we can talk about it intelligently.

Defining Spirituality

The classical definition begins with certain dogmatic and religious presuppositions. For example, prior to recent times spiritual theology was divided into ascetical or ordinary spirituality and mystical or extraordinary spirituality. The assumption was that the latter was reserved for those particularly gifted. There has also been the assumption that there are specific tests of an authentic spiritual life by certain manifestations that accompany it. For example, there are the fruits of the Spirit, such as love, joy, and peace. Or some have insisted that various spiritual epiphenomena must be present, such as speaking in tongues.

The definition of spirituality in this study is generic and experiential. Inasmuch as spirituality is a theological discipline, it reflects the conviction that theology moves from humanity to God and not from God to humanity. This is often described as doing theology "from below." The distinction becomes clear when a generic and experiential definition of spirituality is contrasted with a classical definition.

I have no desire necessarily to pass a negative judgment on the classical definition of spirituality, whatever it may be; but there is a value in beginning with a generic and experiential definition. It permits the widest possible ground for dialogue, since it seeks to begin with the observable data. Furthermore, this definition permits the development of a correspondence with the human sciences although it will quickly move beyond the capabilities of those sciences. In other words, a generic and experiential definition is consistent with a foundational theology that argues for a continuity between nature and supernature.

With this in mind I am defining *spirituality* as (1) a human capacity for relationship (2) with that which transcends sense phenomena; this relationship (3) is perceived by the subject as an expanded or heightened consciousness independent of the subject's efforts, (4) is given substance in the historical setting, and (5) exhibits itself in creative action in the world.

First, there are not two classes of people: those who are spiritual and those who are not. Spirituality is our openness to relationship, which is a universal human capacity involving the whole person. One priest spoke of this very directly:

> Spirituality is a total part of my life. I am a person who is concerned with realities and spirituality is as much a part of that as my right hand and my feelings and my perceptions. It is an appetite which I need to feed.

Plato said that *to be* is *to be in relation* and Aristotle defined the human being as a political animal, *zōē politikē*. This term is sometimes translated "social animal," but it literally means a creature who lives in a city *(polis)*. In other words, for us to be we must exist in a community, in which our identity does not stop with our skin, but extends into the corporate reality. We are our community or the multiple communities of which we are a part.

In the evolutionary process there is a movement from creatures whose behavior is totally intra-specific (i.e., the result of genetic coding), as in an amoeba, to those whose behavior is a reflection of an acquired memory overlaying biology, as in human beings. Culture is the carrier of this memory, and the individual appropriates the cultural memory by socialization within the immediate family and the society as a whole. The supreme example of cultural memory is language, which enables us to be self-conscious and consequently human. This is to say that *Homo sapiens* is a creature with the capacity to think about thinking, to transcend himself or herself, which is made possible by the ability to represent and retain the memory of experience by means of language and to reflect upon that representation with more language.

There is an abiding legend in the folklore of some cultures of the child abandoned by its parents and brought up by wild animals. For some reason the favorite animals are wolves, perhaps harking back to the story of the founders of Rome, Romulus and Remus, who were supposedly suckled by a wolf. Despite romantic speculations to the contrary, the "wolf child" is subhuman because it has not had a relationship with other humans. As a matter of fact, even if such a creature returned to the company of its own kind after a period of years, it would not be able to recapture its lost previous relationships. It would be forever less than human. The evidence in the human sciences that this would be so is overwhelming.

Spirituality begins with this fact that the human being is by nature a creature requiring relationship. It operates from the postulate that to be a person is to be open to the other and goes on to say that there is within each of us an innate longing for union with the other. This urge is known as *eros*, from which we get the word "erotic." But this desire is far more profound than a spicy feeling. It is the fundamental need we have for one another and ultimately for God. It is an energy within us, which, while perhaps deflected in its true end (what the doctrine of original sin seeks to say), is nonetheless a grounding for humanity's spiritual longing.

The human need for relationship is not satisfied by external proximity alone; it is not enough to touch. We must compenetrate, which is to say enter into the internal reality of the other, which requires that we share our inner self. This is the nature of intimacy: to come to know one another as we truly are—or come as close as we can. To put it more graphically, there is a desire to get inside each other's skin, of which sexual intercourse is the most profound symbol.

Yet we never do finally comprehend the other! In every relationship we must eventually come face to face with the mystery of the other person. There is no "solution" to the inquiry, Who are you? For we do not even know who we ourselves are. If we chose to answer the inquirer, we could not. Every human personality is rooted in the mystery of God, and attempts to "explain" humankind ultimately founder because they are inevitably reductions. Most of the self is hidden beneath the surface, reaching into the depths, of God's infinite purpose.

It is only an incredibly vapid culture, like our own, that could permit a theory of human nature to prevail that does not understand this mystery of being. A person is far more than the vortex of his or her material conditioning. Behaviorism, the theory that people can be explained in terms of conditioned reflexes, then, is a reductionism so patently contrary to our everyday experience of the mystery of the being of the other that it is difficult to see how anyone can take it seriously.

This leads, second, to the expectation of spirituality for relationship with that which transcends sense phenomena. If anything characterizes modernity, it is the loss of faith in transcendence, that reality that not only encompasses but surpasses our daily affairs. We have been seduced by our socialization into thinking that all truth is susceptible to scientific analysis (as in the natural sciences). Such analysis reduces all experience to numbers, which are then manipulated in the service of objectivity, prediction, and control. But these three values are incapable of explaining the mystery of human relationship. The fact of the matter is that scientific methodology does not describe reality or any part of it; it only builds models, which are subject to constant revision and are occasionally contradictory to one another.

Spirituality's experience of transcendence is one of being addressed from beyond the material world by that which is greater than anything we on our own can conceive. In the quest of eros for the knowledge of the other we become aware of the fact that the more we know, the more there is to be known. Every answer generates another question or series of questions. There is an infinite presence of the not-yet-known that engages the horizon of our knowing and yet recedes before our inquiry into infinite mystery. The very limits of our language in describing experience leave the questioning person with a sense that "of what we cannot speak we must remain silent"—to quote the philosopher Ludwig Wittgenstein (1889–1951)—and yet in expectant awe.

The transcendence that addresses us is an energy that takes certain forms. In other words, we do not know God in himself, but only as his transcendent being confronts our finite minds. God is the ultimate source of our intrinsic and normative values, but we perceive this as his energy moves in our world. The purpose of life is that final cause embedded in this transcendent presence, always calling us out of where we are to where we might be. It gives global and personal meaning, but that meaning is still penultimate. The transcendent presence imparts to life its quality, as opposed to its quantity. Numbers may point to what lies beyond, but they never encompass this mystery that overcomes the banality of brute facts. It is the character of the spiritual life to be open to this transcendent energy in all its forms.

The notion of transcendence subverts the idea, of course, that all of reality is reducible to the phenomena or the appearances of things. In fact, when science understands itself, there is every indication that its own methodology becomes spiritual (i.e., open to a relationship with what transcends the phenomena). This is to say that the explanation of the methodology of the natural sciences requires that it draw on that which addresses us from outside the material world. There is good evidence that the data resulting from our observations cannot find a coherent and unified resolution in relation to data themselves, but only by reference to a point beyond the data. If seeing alone were believing, as we sometimes suggest, then the world of natural science would be a hopeless morass of contradictions. Transcendence is the hope for meaning we cannot otherwise have, and spirituality is our capacity for a relationship to that meaning: the mind of God.

Third, the key to the identification of the spiritual experience is a heightened or expanded consciousness. This has been the notion guiding much of the research in recent decades in transcendental experience among sociologists of religion, and it is confirmed by the comments among the members of the research sample for this study. For example, one pastor spoke of spiritual awareness as "anything that builds and holds a sense of meaning in life." Another described a new "consciousness" as "something God did for me. It was there and [I] opened up to it. God did it." Still further, a priest spoke of a spiritual turning point as the "clarity of one's call." One pastor's spiritual journey was highlighted by a book, a person, and therapy, which gave his life and discipline "a whole new sense of meaning and purpose."

This sense of a new awareness is at the heart of the Christian spiritual tradition. Teresa of Avila (1515–1582) says of her own mystical experience, which she calls rapture, "What I know in this case is that the soul was never so awake to the things of God nor did it have such a deep enlightenment and knowledge of his Majesty."[1] Among the early church fathers the sacraments, particularly Baptism, are spoken of as the illumination.

David Bohm, a theoretical physicist teaching at the University of London, in a book called *Wholeness and the Implicate Order*,[2] advances the theory that reality is essentially energy, which surrounds us in a flux and flow. This energy, he argues, takes two forms: material reality and consciousness. Consequently, the stuff of creation possesses an implicate or enfolded order that is consciousness. Theological reflection upon this hypothesis suggests that God is present in his creation supremely as one to be known. If we are related to the living God our initial realization of this relationship is in the form of knowledge.

Coming to knowledge, awakening, and illumination are all words or phrases that indicate ourselves as passive recipients. Spirituality is not acquisitive. This is why, in one sense, it is not something we "do." There is nothing that we can *possess* by "being spiritual." It is receptivity, a waiting, a trusting. Whatever knowledge may come does so as a given, over which we have no power or control. It is not a form of problem solving, which is why some may think of it as antithetical to social action. The reason for this passivity is that we have no leverage on the knowledge. We cannot get behind it to grasp it; we have to be open and wait for it. But it is an active passivity, by which I mean that we actually seek to allow the possibility of God's illumination of our heart and minds.

We are aware of the divine energy in perceiving new knowledge. This is what John of the Cross (1542–1591) means when he says that the Word of God is the effect upon the soul. The soul possesses, of course, the mind or what I have described as the capability for the un-contingent process of knowing. When we know God, when the rela-tionship with the transcendent is occurring, the perceivable effect is a heightened or expanded consciousness. In this sense God speaks and we hear his Word.

This approach follows from the understanding that spirituality is rooted in the dynamic of knowing and being known. The participation of the finite subject in the infinite God is in terms of the process of coming into knowledge. But the awareness of that process means it must become incarnate; it must be the form of concrete knowledge, however that may manifest itself. This is analogous to the creative process, which is not recognizable except in works of art, music, sculp-ture, poetry, and the like. Of course, just as the profundity of the cre-ative process is measured by the quality of what it creates, so is our spirituality evaluated by the quality of the awareness that arises.

Fourth, this leads to the substance of that knowledge and the fact that it is always historical. By "historical" is meant that the shape of the content of knowledge is a function of a particular time and place. The Old Testament notion of God, for example, reflects the memory and language of the Hebrew people. The task of Paul was to translate the preaching of Jesus into the culture of the Roman Empire. This in-evitably and appropriately gave our knowledge of God revealed in Christ a distinctive shape.

Generally speaking, Baptists do not have visions of the Blessed Vir-gin, Norwegians do not think of Christ as black, and Muslims do not quote Buddha. We frame our experience of God in those representa-tions that are not only available to us, but particularly deeply ingrained in our memory. The deeper we draw from our memory the greater the power of our knowledge. If I can evoke the Christ of my childhood to help me understand God's presence, it will have far more impact on my life than what I may read about Christ in the latest book.

All this has a great deal to say, of course, about the understanding of spirituality in general in relation to specifically Christian spirituality. God transcends history. He is not in himself a Jew or Christian, any more than he is male or female. The God revealed in Christ is not, as he is to himself, a first-century Jew. The truth that the Christian holds as distinct from other forms of spirituality lies beyond the historical manifestation of God in Christ. For example, God is personal, loving, and forgiving. Even those concepts have a historical quality but certainly reach beyond a temporal and geographical provincialism.

A distinction of Christian spirituality is its willingness to affirm the historical nature of the knowledge of God as something positive. The belief in the Incarnation frees the Christian from the attempt to escape history. There is in Christianity the scandal of particularity, a catch phrase that calls to mind that the identification of God in a moment in history is an invitation to see God in all history. In the historical Jesus we have that supreme moment, the proleptic event of universal history; but it is still history. Human beings are spiritual creatures, therefore, who realize their spirituality in a historical setting.

Fifth, the making of decisions and the action that grows out of those decisions is a product of the knowledge to which we have come. One cannot play tennis unless he first knows there is a game of tennis and is familiar with its rules. A person cannot travel from New York to San Francisco unless she first knows there is a San Francisco and where it lies in relation to New York.

Every action, by which I mean anything we do in which we have a degree of choice (salivation is not an action but a reaction; writing this book is an action), is a projection into the future of what we know about the world. If in the spiritual quest it is true that God expands our consciousness and we know as we did not know before, then inevitably it shows itself in our actions. This is why it is contradictory to say that authentic spirituality is an escape from social action, if in truth God intends that his Kingdom come on this earth as it is in heaven.

For this reason a prophet is a mystic in action. His vision of what should be, if it is of God, can only come from God. It is our spiritual nature that enables us to see and know the world as it is in God's mind and as he intended it to be. Therefore, the fulfillment of a person's spirituality is measured by his or her action on behalf of the Kingdom. By their fruits, Jesus told us, we shall know them.

Ignatius Loyola (1491–1556), the father of modern spiritual theology, speaks to this fifth point. He explains that the purpose of contemplation is to attain the love of God, and then calls attention to two points:

1. Love ought to manifest itself in deeds rather than in words.
2. Love consists in the mutual sharing of goods, for example, the lover gives and shares with the beloved what he possesses, or something of that which he is able to give; and vice versa, the beloved shares with the lover. Hence, if one has knowledge, he shares it with the one who does not possess it; and so also if one has honors, or riches. Thus, one always gives to the other.3

Spiritual theology is, therefore, logically prior to moral theology. Yet it is also a consequence of a moral conversion, the willingness to ask questions of value and to be open to a transcendent vision of the world.

Prayer as Spiritual Action

Prayer is often used as a synonym for spirituality. People who ask how your spirituality is mean to inquire about the state of your prayer life. It is necessary for this discussion to make a distinction between prayer and spirituality, to define prayer, and to explore kinds of prayer. There is no final authority to which to appeal in arriving at these distinctions. They must be drawn selectively from the tradition and our contemporary experience.

In my judgment *prayer* is to spirituality as eating is to hunger. Spirituality is an inner disposition toward a relation with him who transcends the appearances, and prayer is the action this begets. We pray because we are spiritual beings. Those people who do not pray are not "aspiritual"; they choose not to exercise their spirituality and could be said to be spiritually undernourished.

In turn, the desire for God is fed by the act of prayer. We become aware of our spiritual selves as we actively seek to enter into relationship with God. It is like someone who has not eaten for a long time. She may remark after her first bite or two that she did not know how hungry she was until she started to eat. In a similar vein, another may remark that he did not know how much he longed for his wife until he experienced their marriage. Prayer awakens our spirituality.

But this is not to say what prayer is. Our understanding of the meaning of prayer has very much to do with our understanding of God. The New Testament common verbs for prayer, *euchomai* and more especially *proseuchomai*, mean to pray as to wish for something. The implication is that God is the source of what we might desire and prayer consists largely of a "wish list." Such an understanding of prayer raises all kinds of questions about God, if we understand him as he who foreordains all things and knows all that shall come to pass. It is as if one prayed each day for the sun to rise the next. It is almost presumptuous, unless we assume that God chooses for the sun to rise each day by some capricious whim.

Prayer obviously means more than filing our wishes with God. In his treatise *On Prayer*, Origen (c.185–254), one of the greatest minds of the early church, struggles with this question. He believes that to be rational, we have to be free to make choices, but the freedom of humankind operates at a different level than the providence of God. One might say he defines God's providence as the divine vision for his creation. God is no capricious deity and prayer is more than the uplifting of a wish list to him. It is in prayer that the freedom of humankind meets the vision of God. In this act of meeting, humanity is drawn up into the divine purpose. One priest with whom I spoke said, "Prayer is a part of myself and the way I relate to things around me." This points to prayer as a way of seeing creation with God as out eyes.

Prayer is the movement of God to humanity and humanity to God, the act of meeting. It is no less nor is it anything different from that. In whatever manner this meeting is realized it is an act of prayer. In other words, prayer is communication within the relationship between humankind and God and flows both ways. Benedict of Nursia (c.480–550), in his reform of the religious life of the Western church, sought to dignify manual labor as worthy of the monk. He pointed out that to labor is to pray. This makes sense of Paul's injunction that we pray without ceasing (1 Thess. 5:17), for it vastly broadens the context of relationship with God. Prayer is the act of making whatever we do a cause for meeting and knowing God.

Clearly prayer in this sense has as its primary goal not the favorable reply to our requests but the establishment of a relationship. We miss the point of those passages in the Gospels that assure us of the power of prayer if we do not see that they point first of all to the relationship that the follower of Christ has with God. Luke writes, "Even if he will not provide for him out of friendship, the very shamelessness of the request will make him get up and give him all he needs" (Luke 11:8). But God is not only our friend, Luke tells us, he is to us as a loving father. He will give us his Holy Spirit (Luke 11:13): God present, disclosing himself to us and fulfilling our inchoate longing for him.

Not all forms of prayer, however, are the same. For centuries there have been efforts to distinguish different ways in which we pray, if for no other reason than to provide some standard by which to examine our own prayer life. Traditionally the distinction has been made between mental prayer and vocal prayer. The difference here lies in the focused articulation of words, sentences, and paragraphs directed toward God as opposed to the absence of such focus. A meditation on the Annunciation would be mental prayer. A prayer for the return of Aunt Susie's health would be vocal prayer.

It is better to distinguish forms of prayer by a less mechanical means that would allow for a less arbitrary or artificial division. I would suggest that the different kinds of prayer fall along a *continuum of focused intentionality on the part of the person who prays*. At one end of this continuum is prayer that intends to intend nothing at all; at the other end of the continuum there is prayer that intends a specific answer from God, for example, the healing of Aunt Susie, the safe return from a journey, the forgiveness of our sins.

It is apparent that as persons mature spiritually their prayers move from a more to a less focused intentionality. Classically this has been described as a movement toward contemplation and union with God. Richard of St. Victor (d. 1173) defines contemplation as "the free, more penetrating gaze of a mind, suspended with wonder concerning manifestations of wisdom."[4] There is nothing so extraordinary in what he means. An analogy might be the quiet communion that can take place between persons in a close, longstanding marriage. For example, my youngest child has, since his older siblings left home, complained of the silence in our home. My wife and I sometimes sit or drive together, saying nothing for hours. Our son will interrupt when he can bear it no longer and ask if we are angry with one another. When we reply in the negative, he then asks what we were thinking about. Often we have to say, "Nothing." Yet there is a specific desire to be with one another and the quality of silence together is indeed different from the quality of silence alone.

There are forms of prayer that have as their purpose the inducement of this state. They work on the principle that by means of simplicity and repetition the mind is emptied of worldly concerns and becomes open to the transcendent Word. The Jesus prayer—"Jesus Christ, Son of God, Savior, have mercy upon me"—repeated over and over in rhythm with our breathing is an example. It has an honored history of over fifteen hundred years, but it is only one example of a genre of prayer, both Christian and non-Christian, that has the purpose of enabling us to intend nothing at all in the act of prayer. Any such prayer whose purpose is to empty the mind of images is called apophatic prayer.

Physical exercise, manual labor or jogging, for example, can also have an apophatic effect in prayer. There is an unfocused openness that can occur in this kind of activity that, when we consciously direct the experience, can allow for an awareness of God's presence to emerge. The same thing can happen in any routine task, such as driving on an interstate highway, that engages the more automatic level of consciousness and leaves the higher brain functions relatively free.

Prayer that lies at the less focused end of the continuum is in a listening mode. The aim is not to tell God what we wish, much less to inform him of the weather, world events, or of the little crises at home. In that curious mixture of sensory metaphors common to spiritual theology, we listen that we might see. A spiritual friend of mine describes sitting on a high place in a field and listening to the wind until it forms an image in her mind. This is a way of saying that prayer for her is an imaginative attending to what is beyond mere sense data.

Contemplation is not the same thing as meditation. Meditation is more focused in its intention than contemplation, although it still seeks to listen. The early Benedictines spoke of the *lectio divina*, "divine reading." There is nothing esoteric about this. What they meant was that we ought to read the Scriptures and books of spiritual merit in a slow and deliberate fashion, chewing over each sentence and paragraph for whatever message may be there. Later a whole methodology of meditation was built upon this and made popular by Ignatius Loyola and, even more, by the French spiritual masters of the seventeenth century such as Francis de Sales (1567–1622) and Jean-Jacques Olier (1608–1657).

Meditation that customarily draws upon scriptural imagery to be a "carrier" of the divine message in prayer is a kataphatic form of prayer. By this I mean that it requires an overt and imaginative retention of certain images. The one who prays plays with them, much as one might play with a kaleidoscope. There is no expectation of a given pattern that might emerge, but attention is paid to whatever pattern appears. It becomes a source of spiritual listening in order, to mix the metaphor once more, that one might see.

A number of the clergy interviewed in this research center their prayer in a meditative reading of Scripture. Certainly this conforms to the Reformation principle that if the individual comes to the Bible prayerfully, the Holy Spirit will illumine his or her understanding of what is read. There is nothing so formal as the principles of Jesuit or French methodology, but the intent is very much the same.

At the more focused end of the continuum of prayer is what has customarily been called verbal prayer. The Lord's Prayer is verbal prayer, as are the *Gloria in excelsis* and the Hail Mary. The one who prays is telling God what he or she has in mind. Such prayer has been divided into a number of classes of telling and these in themselves are of varying focus. For our purposes here, moving from lesser to greater focus, I will list five classes of such prayer: adoration, thanksgiving, confession, intercession, and petition.

Adoration is an act of love and praise. It is like telling a spouse, "You are the most wonderful man (or woman) in the world." It is akin to a football cheer. Obviously, what we expect in return is a like feeling. *Thanksgiving* is a recognition of the source of our blessings, and *confession* is an awareness of our failure to love as we claim to love. These three classes of prayer are clearly relational in nature and differ from contemplation and meditation only in the concerted activity of the one who would pray.

Intercession and *petition* are different. They have an end result in mind. It is in reference to such prayer that we struggle with the issue of "unanswered prayer." The great amount of energy spent on the problem of intercession and petition is symptomatic of a failure to appreciate the vast continuum of prayer and its fundamental goal of relationship with God. While there is no doubt some legitimacy to the problem of unanswered prayer in general, most effort has been expended on it vis-à-vis intercession and petition because of their sharply focused intentionality.

Many years ago I was listening to a radio preacher while driving across country. He was explaining the cause of unanswered prayer in some very down-home imagery. As he said, the other day he had tried to call his old grandma, and all he got was static on the telephone. He complained to the telephone company, who explained that a cat had climbed the power pole, been electrocuted, and fallen on the telephone lines between him and his grandma. "If we expect our prayer to be answered," he suggested, "we have to get the 'dead cat' off the lines."

There is a sense in which this anecdote is misleading and another in which it is legitimate. The problem of unanswered prayer is not the result of technological failure. Yet prayer is primarily an act of communication that deepens our relationship with God. If we intend too much, want our own goals and desires too much, these intentions can become the "dead cat" on the lines. We cannot listen and see, because we lack the purity of heart of which Matthew spoke (5:8). Purity of heart is an uncluttered intention to know the will of God. The "dead cats" can be our notions of what ought to be which stand in the way of God's intentions.

Prayer that is not primarily listening always runs the risk of getting in the way of the ultimate purpose of prayer, a deepened sharing in God's vision for his world. This is the supreme lesson of Jesus' prayer on the Mount of Olives: "Father, if it be thy will, take this cup away from me. Yet not my will but thine be done!" (Luke 22:42). In doing God's will we come into relationship with him, which is the ultimate goal of the spiritual life.

This is undoubtedly the reason why growth in the Spirit involves a movement toward a less focused intentionality in prayer, while not requiring a total abrogation of intercession and petition. The surrender of the ego becomes a very real part of prayer and, perhaps, a reason why prayer itself can be frightening—it is built upon trust.

Conclusion

The fundamental assumption of this study is that God created human beings with the capacity for relationship with himself. Spirituality is a disposition and a potentiality for that relationship. It is not a part or piece of humanity, it is a character that cuts through the totality of the human, involving all of the individual; but it points to a particular posture of the person, which is distinguishable from emotional well-being, physical health, or intellectual activity. The key to spirituality is the awareness of a transcendent gift of knowledge.

Whereas spirituality needs to be understood specifically and experientially, prayer requires a broader definition than we often give it. It is the intentional act of entering into a relationship with God. That intention does not have to be focused, however, in any specific way. The key to prayer is the conscious direction of the self to the subject that lies behind and beyond the world as it appears.

In Christian prayer the conscious intention has within it certain symbols, principally the symbol of Christ. This is what it means to pray in the name of Jesus. The manner of our reaching out to God is moved and shaped by our image of our Lord and the infusion of God's Word within our consciousness is substantially Christlike.

2. Spiritual Instrumentality

WHEN I was growing up I was told a story of Joseph B. Cheshire (1850–1932), sometime bishop of the Episcopal Diocese of North Carolina. He had been invited to a formal dinner at the home of the governor of North Carolina, and as the distinguished guests gathered about the table in the state dining room the governor, turning to the bishop, asked, "Would you, sir, please return thanks?" Bishop Cheshire was a man of imposing presence, strong opinion, and direct language. He looked at the governor and replied, "Say it yourself! It's your own house!"

Bishop Cheshire believed that a bishop or any other ordained person, when a guest in someone's home, is just that—a guest and nothing more. Unless he comes exercising some authority pertaining to ordination—for example, celebrating the Eucharist for someone who is ill or blessing the house—the fact of his ordination makes him no more a candidate for offering prayer than any other guest. Cheshire thought that it was appropriate for family members—he would have said the head of the family—to offer prayers within the household.

Yet the governor, like many hosts, somehow thought it right to ask the clergy person present to pray. This is more than simply a common courtesy, in my judgment, and we would err to dismiss it in this way. There is an intuition of the role of the ordained person of which this request was symptomatic that we need to explore. This will require us to develop succinctly a theology of the ordained person. But before that is done, it is necessary to rehearse the evolution of the discipline of spiritual theology.

Ascetical and Mystical Theology

An analytical and systematic theology, as distinct from thinking about religious experience, became a possibility when we became aware of conceptual thought as a model of experience and not as identical with experience. When we understood that language interprets and mediates what happens to us and does not present us with a photographic repre- sentation of what is, then we were free to see that theology operates by its own internal logic. The substance and process of theology is historically conditioned, and it changes from time to time. There is a good reason for saying that analytical and systematic theology came into existence in the thirteenth century when we became aware of the internal logic of philosophical thought as a basis for theology.

The reason for suggesting the thirteenth century is that the adoption of an Aristotelian philosophical approach was for the first time a conscious choice of a logical system among a number of other systems (e.g., Neo-Platonism), which formed a means of interpreting the Christian experience. It would be like today choosing between existential phenomenology, linguistic analysis, or personalism. Few would argue that one of these systems of thought is any more intrinsically Christian than the other.

Within analytical theology spiritual theology arose as a subdiscipline in the sixteenth century, although its roots lie in the twelfth century. It was in Spain that it first developed, but rapidly schools arose in Italy and France as well. English spiritual theology was less systematic.

Two separate areas of focus formed within the overall discipline we now call spiritual theology. One was ascetical theology, which dealt with the spiritual discipline of the ordinary Christian. The word "ascetical" came from the Greek *askēsis*, meaning the practice or training of an athlete. The emphasis is on the action of the Christian to enable himself to be open to God's presence. The other focus was mystical theology, which concerned the gift of God's presence to certain persons possessing the capacity for transcendental experience. The word "mystical" is drawn from the use of the Greek *mustērion* by Dionysius the pseudo-Areopagite (c.500) to name the ascent of the soul to union with God. Although it is not universally taught, the common implication in the division into ascetical theology and mystical theology is that there are two kinds of Christians: those who take the "low road" of asceticism and those given the "high road" of mystical experience.

Certainly no one has ever suggested that the dividing line between the subjects of ascetical theology and those of mystical theology is ordination. There are far too many simple folk, including women and children, from every century who have testified to the mystical experience of God to even contemplate such a possibility.

But now the division itself is generally repudiated. Certainly the generic, experiential definition in spiritual theology implies that whatever the mystical experience may be, it is possible for anyone. It would appear that one basis for the limiting judgment is that the signs of union with God might indeed be too narrowly interpreted. For far too long it was assumed that someone who enjoyed the marriage bed, took baths, owned property, or attended the opera could not have a mystical experience. It is undoubtedly the case that our circumstances influence the fulfillment of our individual capacity for transcendental experience and it appears likely that persons of a more intuitive bent are more likely to discern God's immediate presence in their lives than the more practical. But the possibility is never lacking.

Yet I would not discard altogether a possible interpretation of the distinction between ascetical and mystical theology that makes them helpful categories. Rather than use these terms, however, I would prefer to speak of *instrumental* and *terminal* images in spiritual theology. Ascetical theology had to do with the practice of a Christian discipline, the *means* by which one intended the presence of God in his or her life. Fasting, regular times for prayer, the use of the rosary, Bible reading, and acts of compassion are examples of discipline that the Christian "athlete" may find helpful in opening his or her life to God's Word. They become instrumental images within the intention of the disciple.

Mystical theology had to do with the description of the person's experience of union with God, whether or not this referred to an immediate or mediate relationship. The marriage of the Lamb, the luminous darkness, the soul stripped naked before the abyss, and the heart strangely warmed are descriptive of the goal of prayer. They are, therefore, terminal images, which may or may not appeal to the disciple's intended end.

As we explore the theology of ordination in relation to the spiritual life, it is important that we keep in mind particularly the place of instrumental imagery. This distinction between instrumental images and terminal images may well provide a clue toward a resolution of the uncertain distinction between the spiritual discipline of the priest or pastor and the people of God as a whole.

Our Inheritance

Ordination is the authorization of a person to perform a certain function within the community; it is the bestowal of authority. Inasmuch as the church recognizes the authority of the one ordained, he or she *becomes* the one who possesses that power to act in certain ways. We do not just preach the Gospel, we become the preacher. We do not just possess the authorization to preside at the Eucharist, we become the priest who represents the one, sufficient sacrifice of Christ. We are our community and we are what our community makes us. Our doing becomes our being.

But the manner of ordination or authorization of one to function in a given way varies. Who ordains? Even within the Roman Catholic Church it has not always been a bishop. How do we ordain? Usually by laying on of hands, but the bestowal of a chalice and paten or the clothing in the vestments of the office have served at times and places for the matter of ordination. In the final analysis ordination is an action of the community who ordains, and that community must choose how it may declare a person to be whatever it is he or she is to have authority to do.

It has always been true that there are those within the church who are recognized as possessing a spiritual proficiency that excels what the rest of us have. They have been "ordained" one might say as spiritual masters, as examples and guides to the people of God. They include the desert fathers from the third and fourth centuries, the monks and friars of the Middle Ages, holy women such as Catherine of Siena (1347–1380), Julian of Norwich (d.c.1443), and Catherine of Genoa (1447–1510), and the wandering preachers, known and unknown, of colonial America. Many of these were not ordained persons in the technical sense. They were not priests or pastors whom the church in solemn assembly before God set apart to preach the Word and administer the sacraments. But the people of God knew them by their possessing spiritual gifts. They were holy men and women.

Myron Madden, a Baptist pastor and theologian, has done considerable research in the meaning of blessing. A fundamental point he makes is that the power to bless is given by the one blessed. It is the character of ordination. The person who does the blessing is set apart as an instrument for this purpose and the energy conveyed in blessing comes from God, but the authority to exercise this function is bestowed by those who will be its recipients. This is an important distinction.

In truth we need to remember that prior to the sixteenth century the ministry of the church was much less defined than now and restricted to the clerical caste, that is, those educated and ordained by duly constituted authority. Just about the time Christian scholars wrote long essays on the priesthood of all believers we divided the church into clergy and clients, those who *did* ministry and those who were *done* to. Formal ordination became more and more the only kind of "ordination," save in such unusual circumstances as with the Russian Orthodox starets, a layman who serves as a spiritual counselor because of his obvious holiness.

The effect of this has been to narrow people's expectations of ministerial gifts to those who bear the stamp of approval from the ecclesiastical hierarchy. There has, to all accounts, become only one kind of ordained person, named variously the priest, the pastor, the parson, the preacher, the presbyter, or, unfortunately, the minister. I say unfortunately because all Christians are in fact called to be ministers, and to designate one class by this name is a tacit surrender of the theological understanding of baptism. It is to give in totally to the narrowing of ministerial function into one role, which has progressively characterized Western Christianity for more than four hundred years and has culminated in the last seventy years in the professional model of ministry.

The effect of this reduction of ordination to one class of persons has been to encourage the people of God to attribute to them all ministerial functions. Included in this is the role of spiritual master, the example and guide to the faithful in the journey toward union with God. Fortunately there are exceptions to this attribution, and some very holy men and women who have not been formally ordained can and do function as spiritual masters. Simone Weil (1909–1943), who was never even baptized much less ordained, is a near-contemporary who comes to mind.

Yet there is no doubt that ordained persons today embody people's expectations that they be spiritually proficient in a special way. We would tend to think that the nonordained spiritual guide would be the exception to the rule, which is that ordination solemnizes the gift of holiness. Why else do many folk project their understanding, or more often misunderstanding, of what it is to be holy on the man or woman set apart by the hierarchy as priest or pastor? In what other manner can we explain that most people who experience a call to a specific ministry first seek ordination? The seminary I serve certainly has some students with a vocation to ministry but not to priesthood or even the diaconate.

My research and reflection would suggest that there is a legitimate connection between spiritual proficiency and functional ordination—the recognition formally or informally—of one as embodying a particular authority within the church. Because we today with rare exception conceive of ordination as a formal action of duly constituted authority, this relationship between spiritual proficiency and ordination needs to be discussed in terms of the institution's priest or pastor. But I want to make clear that there is no theological reason why it must be so. It is the result of a historical process, which many of us wish were otherwise.

When I speak of the ordained person, therefore, the reader might well consider the boundaries of that definition as not altogether congruent with the clerical registers of a particular denomination or denominations. Like Antony of Egypt (c.251–356), Evagrius Ponticus (346–399), Teresa of Avila (1515–1582), George Fox (1624–1691), and countless others—none of whom ever made it to the presbyterate, but all of whom were Christian spiritual giants—there are those today upon whom no one has laid hands, but who possess great gifts as spiritual guides and examples.

Symbol and Symbol-Bearer

"The priest can live the lifestyle that most people in the parish cannot and wish they could. We are in a sense cast in an almost vicarious role." These are the words of a priest asked the difference between clerical and lay spirituality. What he did not say, but what is implied by his statement, is that at the heart of the ordained ministry is an intangible power of presence that I would describe as the function of symbol and symbol-bearer.

The priest or pastor objectifies in his or her person and by what he or she does as the one preaching and presiding at the liturgy a constellation of images that serves as a symbol of God's presence. I have argued this at some length elsewhere[1] and here only intend to summarize what appears to be the case. A symbol, it needs to be borne in mind, represents that which cannot otherwise be grasped, in this case, God. Furthermore, a symbol serves to enable our participation in what it represents. The church and her sacraments are a class of symbols.

I am not implying that ordination effects some kind of internal characterological change in a person. It is not clear what such a change might mean. It does appear true, however, that within the consciousness of a community that recognized a person as ordained and within the awareness of its individual members he or she becomes a symbol. He or she represents and shapes a sense of the divine that wells up from deep within the corporate and individual memories of the people of God.

The frequent identification of the pastor or priest as "God" by small children is a hint of what happens. The authority attributed to the ordained person, sometimes even occult power, can be understood in this light. The violent feelings of some in the presence of ordained women is best explained in the light of the capacity of the clerical symbol to bring to consciousness in the form of projection the buried memories of an individual.

Karl Rahner, probably the twentieth century's most perceptive theologian, explains that the priest is at the core the one who proclaims the Word. But we must be careful not to interpret "proclaim" or "Word" too narrowly. The pastor makes present to our consciousness that which symbolizes the mind of God, which is what "Word" means. He or she does this not just by preaching or teaching, but perhaps even more powerfully in the liturgy, at the sickbed, in the home at occasions of crisis, and just by being there.

William Willimon in an insightful book, *Worship and Pastoral Care*,[2] describes in a helpful manner the role of liturgy as a means of making present God's healing power in a way nothing else can. His understanding of ordination, however, reduces the pastor to a technician with a temporary certificate of competence, issued only reluctantly. He explains his position as opposed to that of Henri Nouwen in *The Wounded Healer*[3] and my own, particularly as explained in *The Future Shape of Ministry*[4] by explaining his own as experiential and ours as "mystical." My reply to this is that Nouwen's and my argument concerning the role of the ordained person is thoroughly consistent with Willimon's understanding of liturgy and necessary for it. Furthermore, I would claim that it is a position that is ultimately both experiential and mystical.

The experience of the ordained person, particularly within the context of that bundle of symbols that constitutes liturgy, is as a mystagogue. A mystagogue is one who leads us into mystery. The mystery lies within ourselves. It has long been a principle of spiritual theology that the knowledge of God lies at the end of self-awareness. "Strain every nerve in every possible way," writes the anonymous fourteenth-century author of *The Cloud of Unknowing*, "to know and experience yourself as you really are. It will not be long, I suspect, before you have a real knowledge and experience of God as he is."[5] The priest or pastor becomes a means of entering into a mystery that is really our own. This is the "vicarious role" of the ordained person.

In some traditions this is why the priest is called the *alter Christus*, the "other Christ." Images of neo-rococo holy cards may well emerge at the thought of the priest as *alter Christus*, because there is a kind of saccharine piety that once collected in the Roman Catholic tradition about ordination and the first Mass of the new priest. Yet behind the impediments there is hidden a truth. The identification of the ordained person within the religious community with his or her function casts that individual into a position that is analogous with the incarnation of God in Christ. When in the Episcopal Church as a result of liturgical renewal it became more the practice of the priest to stand at the altar facing the people, it was frequently objected that his Christ-like function became too personal, too confrontational.

Whereas in the Protestant traditions there has been an effort to separate theologically the person of the pastor from the function of one who preaches the Word and administers the sacraments, it has not worked in practice. There is a symbolic power in the ordained person, no matter what his or her theology. Billy Graham lives in Montreat, North Carolina, behind electrified fences with dogs patrolling the property. This is not the style of life of an egomaniac in this case—it is protection from those who would not only "touch the hem of his garment" at an inopportune moment, but would rip it off his back as a "holy relic."

The power within the ordained person is what in fact the community gives to him or her as a sacrament of Christ, who is in turn the primal sacrament of God. The pastor or priest is rooted in a world of symbols and takes on the character of his or her environment. There is an expectation that gathers about that person which, while not of his or her making, is real. Part of that expectation is that they live into the mystagogic role with their lives. The ordained person is expected to be a person of prayer that the person in the street cannot be.

Several surveys of lay persons about what they look for in the ordained person show this expectation. People speak in various ways of wanting their pastor to be spiritually deep. At the very least this means they want to feel in his or her presence that he or she listens to more than the sirens of secularism—even if they cannot help themselves from being dashed against the values of this present age. Of course, we must sometimes reserve the right to question what is commonly considered evidence of "spiritual depth."

The Hermeneut

Symbol as symbol is characterized by a passive activity. Like a painting in an art museum it speaks to us as we engage it. There is nothing in a painting that could "correct" our participation, because the dialogue is initiated and maintained only by the one engaging the symbol. The more intentional—yet still symbolic—function of the ordained person enables the inner dynamic of the mind's illumination by God, which is hermeneutic process. A symbol as hermeneut possesses an active passivity.

Hermeneutics within theology is the discipline of interpretation. It refers usually to the interpretation of the Bible, its exegesis and application to life; but it can typically also refer to the reflection upon any other sacred text (e.g., creeds, liturgies, and doctrinal definitions). But the word hermeneutics has more life to it than this. It comes from the name of a Greek god, Hermes, who was the messenger between humans and the gods.

Sometimes thought of as androgynous, Hermes was the trickster. He was a maverick, weird, full of surprises, and a bit irreverent. In ancient Greece his image, replete with an erect phallus, guarded the entrance of the typical Athenian house. Hermes was considered the guardian of travelers, merchants, and thieves. It is from such a strange figure that we get our word for the solemn activity of interpreting the meaning of sacred texts.

Several things suggest themselves in the light of the enigmatic Hermes. First, Hermes subverts the presumptions of humankind. He never lets us assume that things are as they appear to be. The hermeneutic function of the priest or pastor may well begin with this task of subverting the assumptions of people. We live in a particularly secular age, but even the most religious period in history is given to constructing a collective consciousness in which God occupies a prescribed category. Such a domesticated deity does not call us out to the spiritual pilgrimage. He legitimates where we already are.

One of the prevailing interpretations of the parables of Jesus is that our Lord told them for the purpose of subverting our worldview. Despite the fact that parables such as the good Samaritan (Luke 20:29–37), the prodigal son (Luke 15:11–24), the Pharisee and the tax-gatherer (Luke 18:9–14), and the landowner who employed laborers for his vineyard (Matt. 20:1–16) are so familiar to us, if we read them in this light they do in fact challenge the basic assumptions of value within society. Christ was weird; he did not fit in. And those who would be "other Christs" should draw a clue from him. This is not a weirdness for its own sake, but an incongruity that is both a result and a cause of the Gospel's mission to call us out on pilgrimage.

Second, Hermes does not carry his own message. The hermeneut, the one who as interpreter represents God to humankind and humankind to God, is an instrument of knowing, not the source. Christ is the sacrament of God. In the incarnation the manifest humanity of Jesus does not face us with an immediate confrontation with the Godhead. He is the glory of God, the veiled presence. Christ *mediates* between God and humanity. The Fourth Evangelist has Jesus saying as much: "The teaching that I give is not my own; it is the teaching of him who sent me" (John 7:16). If it is true that the ordained person participates in this sacramentality of Christ, then far more is it true that the authority of her or his office is derivative from God and he or she is only called to mediate.

But that mediation is vital. The myth of Hermes captures an essential reality of our existence. We come to know ourselves, even our inner selves, as we reflect on the data of our experience with another. It is as if we can only hear the word of God by its being reflected in a mirror. Although God speaks, we cannot hear until it is reflected to us by the hermeneut, the person tangibly present to us. It is not the ordained person's message, and he or she may not even be aware of what we are hearing.

An illustration of this is the sermon. There is not a preacher who has not experienced over and over again people thanking him for what they heard. I have had people tell me "my message" changed their lives, and when I ask what I might have said it is something I was never conscious of having said. The message belonged to the hearer and I was only an instrument in its mediation.

Third, Hermes traveled a dangerous road. According to Greek mythology, chaos, the vast, confused, turbulent sea of primordial matter, lay between the gods and humanity. Chaos is not synonymous with evil here; its danger lies in the fact that it is undifferentiated. We are only comfortable in a world in which things have boundaries and we can deal with them in expected, finite ways. Chaos is quite the opposite: unpredictable and uncontrollable.

It is the road through chaos that the hermeneut, priest or pastor, travels in the company of those he or she serves. One does not have to be long in the work of spiritual direction to discover the nature of this path. A person presents himself to the pastor and asks for help on the spiritual journey. The first real step along the way is often the wrenching task of naming the demons that arise as soon as the two set out into the unfamiliar territory of the interior life.

A fundamental measure for evaluating genuine movement in the spiritual life is the presence of strong, *mixed* emotions—joy and horror, fascination and fear, delight and desolation—which are typical of the inner wilderness. I recall early in my ministry someone who came seeking a clearer knowledge of the way to holiness and was greatly distressed to find that she could not merely put behind her a life of bizarre sexual experience but had to confront its possible meaning for her—both negative and positive. "Why," she asked, "cannot that lie buried in my past?" It cannot be "buried" because it is there. Also, a friend of mine, who genuinely loved the Lord and believed that he was following the simple Gospel of Christ, was deeply shaken to discover that it was not enough. His fellow Christians still set out to destroy him when what he did infringed upon their self-interests. "Satan himself masquerades as an angel of light" (2 Cor. 11:14). The will of God is rarely obvious to us ourselves, much less to others.

I recall once at a clergy conference asking the rhetorical question of those attending: "How do you spend your time?" One man, to my surprise, answered: "Helping people get through the night!" But pastors have no infrared vision; it is just as dangerous for them to walk the path in the night as it is for the persons they accompany—and a little more frightening, because they know how risky it is. Once and for all we need to lay aside every notion that the prayer life is easy or sure. The trail is marked with the spiritual graves of those who thought it was.

Furthermore, the system does not often reward the hermeneut. In presenting this model to clergy I have generally found it congruent with their self-image but at the same time seen it raise anxieties. It presents a frightening image to the people who chose their pastors and who want someone who can assure them of the availability of cheap grace. There is a certain bitterness abroad when it comes to being

honest to the hermeneutical function and still trying to find that support which makes the ordained life tolerable.

The Instrumental Image

An inevitable loneliness accompanies the service of the pastor. I do
not mean that the ordained person must by the fact of his or her office
keep apart from persons, aloof and unsullied. Quite the contrary! He
or she as symbol and hermeneut becomes an intimate part of the inner life of those who know him or her and risks the misunderstanding,
the caricature, and the rejection that may emerge from the image
evoked. The loneliness is of a different kind.

One of the more remarkable interviews in this study involved a
pastor who was for three years a captive of the Chinese Communists
right after they took over mainland China. His account of facing death
every day and of experiencing their constant efforts to break his faith
was more than fascinating; it was deeply moving. Toward the end of
his time there he was held in a hotel, cut off from contact with all other
Christians, utterly alone. As he described it, "All the things that I believed, which were true, were put on the anvil and beaten very hard."
What sustained him during those horrible months was the disciplined
study of Holy Scripture.

Very few of us will ever have to experience that kind of loneliness,
but ordination does indeed place us upon the anvil of people's expectations to be beaten out. I think of Jesus' words to Simon Peter, "Satan has been given leave to sift all of you like wheat" (Luke 22:31). No
one wants to be used, but the vocation of the ordained is to be used as
an instrument for the spiritual awakening of humankind. The pastor
or priest becomes a part of the *askesis* of those among whom he finds
himself.

The missionary to China, sitting in one room with a couple of his
captors reading his Bible, becomes to them the symbol and hermeneut
of the God who sent his son to give his life for humankind. Passively active and actively passive, his life is not his own to come or to go; he can
only let it be to those about him what they will. But herein lies his integrity. It is a life grounded in the Christ whose story is told in the Scriptures. What effect it may have, however, we can only leave to God, who
himself gives the freedom to us to use the ordained person as we will.

Two implications follow from this. The first is that the pastor's work is not accomplished by his ability to control those to whom he or she is called to minister. Herein lies a source of frustration. There is some evidence that persons seeking ordination may have higher than usual dominance need. This is to say that there is a need to be in charge and that at some level of consciousness the clerical role is perceived as a means of fulfilling that need. There may be fantasies of preaching to a captive audience and "telling them how it is." I recall an Episcopal priest, foiled again and again in his efforts to get his congregation to do what he thought they should, standing in the pulpit explaining that the title "rector" comes from the Latin meaning "ruler." Yet the power of the vocation lies in the willingness of the ordained to let happen what will happen.

Here is where a more feminine consciousness could help—in men a more androgynous personality. In our research sample of spiritually mature male clergy, it is noteworthy that according to the Bem Sex Role Inventory (BSRI), although a feminine consciousness is differentiated in every instance, often less than a point distinguishes between it and a masculine consciousness, and in several instances the feminine consciousness exceeds the masculine. When this is compared to Bem's own research, it is noted that the percentage of men measuring as androgynous (the two scales within a point of one another), 78 percent, far exceeds her two samples of 34 percent and 44 percent.[6] In a conference advertised for the "spiritually mature," including both clergy and laity, I discovered that 100 percent of the women attending scored androgynous or feminine, compared to 86 percent in both of Bem's samples, and the men attending scored 67 percent androgynous or feminine, compared to 45 percent and 65 percent in Bem's two samples.[7] Of course, those persons were self-selecting.

Ralph Hood and James Hall, in research exploring the relationship between men and women reporting mystical experiences and the use of agenitive (e.g., as to enter the divine presence) or receptive (e.g., as to *empty* oneself in order to receive God) images, discovered that it is clear that women use receptive language. The problem is that men are confused. Agenitive images do not work very well with the Western view of a masculine God and consequently men tend to use receptive language as well. Because of the male self-identity, however, men are inhibited in this regard and consequently they have mystical experiences, which seem to require a feminine imagery, less frequently than women.[8] This would be consistent with the theory that the spiritual capacity of a person is activated largely through a feminine consciousness and adds more support to the subtle encouragement of this dimension of the ordained person.

This leads to the second implication of the instrumentality of the priest or pastor. It is that he or she does not "elect" to become an aid to the spiritual growth of those who recognize him or her as ordained, but inevitably functions as a symbol or diabol in those persons' spiritual journeys. A diabol is the antonym of a symbol; it destroys what the symbol edifies. The instrumentality of the ordained functions independently of their choice.

This is the message of Graham Greene's novel *The Power and the Glory*, recounting the story of the "whiskey priest" in Mexico and his unwilling martyrdom; it is the tragedy of those who have lost their sense of vocation and yet serve as pastors. How well I recall the rector of a well-known parish saying to me with a mind loosened a bit by several stiff drinks, half joking and half sobbing, "Why do they think I can help them find God? Sometimes I wake up in the morning and do not know whose bed I am in."

What follows in the balance of this study does not come under the heading of elective study. It is an exploration of the ways in which a priest or pastor may live out that instrumentality in the spiritual lives of the people he or she serves. The ordained person in fact becomes those instrumental images. Only when we understand this will we begin to plumb the power of such a ministry and acknowledge the strong feelings—negative as well as positive—that attach themselves to the priest or pastor.

Conclusion

One of the persons interviewed for this study remarked, "I certainly see myself in the priesthood as partly the intercessor for the parish. That provokes a lot of guilt in me, because . . . I do not think of that aspect of my priesthood enough." The phrase "my priesthood" calls itself to my attention. There are those who believe that it is a presumptuous way of speaking, for there is only one priesthood, that of Christ, in which he graciously permits us to share—and theologically this is correct.

But I have been present among fellow clergy and heard them speak of their priesthood and as I have listened it does not strike me as presumptuous. They know whose priesthood they share, but they are saying something more. They are speaking of a commitment to be instruments of God's Word, evoking a new awareness in the lives of those they serve. They speak of "my priesthood" as both a curse and a blessing, but also an indissolvable reality. Even among the majority of the persons interviewed who insist there is no difference between clerical and lay spirituality, there is a sense in which they have been called to this ministry before they were formed in the womb (Jer. 1:5). All low doctrines of the ordained ministry miss this point, which is as real to those who are called as the Lord they serve.

To be an intercessor is to be this instrument of new awareness, for intercession is not so much getting what you ask as it is a coming into the knowledge of him of whom we would ask. It is the first step in a deepening awareness of the God who searches us out that he might love us.

3. The Sins of the Clergy

THE FATHERS of the early church who went out into the desert are popularly thought to have been fleeing the evils of civilization. But this is a simplification. They thought of themselves more properly as going out to fight evil. The demons, as well as the angels, were believed to live in the wilderness and there could be confronted and bested in all their horrible destructiveness.

The besetting sin of the desert fathers was acedia or *accidie*, tellingly described as "the devil of the noonday sun." Acedia is spiritual boredom, an indifference to matters of religion, or simple laziness. Symeon the New Theologian wrote to his monks, "Do not forget your special tasks and your handicraft to walk about aimlessly and in dissipation and so expose yourselves to the demon of accidie."[1] His remark is almost a commentary on the axiom, "Idle hands are the devil's workshop."

The ancient sin of acedia lies at the root of the pastor's or priest's refusal to heed the calling to be the instrument of spiritual growth. In 1977 Carlyle Marney, a distinguished Baptist "pastor to pastors," spoke at the seminary where I serve. I remember him asking our students if they thought after ten years they would still love the Lord Jesus or if instead would have become "hand tamed by the gentry." Of course, he would have been exceedingly surprised if any had confessed that probably the latter would be the case, but the fact is that many ordained persons quickly lose a sense of the excitement of the spiritual quest. They succumb to acedia in those forms that are to a degree peculiar to our times, and yet share much with previous centuries of clergy.

Many of us when we think of the sins of the clergy recall the "fallen priest" in literature, such as the Reverend T. Lawrence Shannon in Tennessee Williams' play, *The Night of the Iguana*. He was a boozer, a wencher, and had lost his faith. Yet, such a person is less a sinner than he is a casualty. American religion is obsessed with the "warm sins" such as illicit sex and gluttony. Because many of us are Donatists—believing that the validity of the sacrament depends upon the moral character of its minister, which was condemned as a heresy long ago—we become inordinately concerned when the warm sins are committed by the ordained. What we fail to realize is that pastor or priest who succumbs to the sins of passion is fallen in the same manner as a fallen soldier. These are the demons that threaten anyone who sets out upon the path through chaos. Some will lose.

The sins that should concern us far more deeply are those that prevent the ordained from ever exercising their spiritual vocation. These "cold sins" truly violate the mission of the pastor to be a symbol, symbol-bearer, and hermeneut. They arise not from an excess of passion, but from a fear of passion. They are the product of a calculated apathy, sustained only by the embers of a dying soul.

Acedia is the root sin of the clergy as spiritual guides. Like a cancer it eats away at our abandonment to the love for God and his creation. It takes a number of forms, which have much in common with those of other centuries but also have their own peculiar twist in our times.

The Lust for Power

Everyone needs to possess power. Power is the ability to change situations and circumstances. The issue is not the fact of power per se, but rather the nature and source of that power.

The Greek word for power, *dunamis* (we get the word "dynamite" from it), is common in the New Testament, as is a word for authority, *exousia*, which is sometimes translated as power. There power is of God and is given to the church that creation might become whole. Jesus before his ascension tells the apostles, "You will receive power when the Holy Spirit comes upon you; and you will bear witness for me . . . away to the ends of the earth" (Acts 1:8). Paul declares that the Gospel "is the saving power of God for everyone who has faith" (Rom. 1:16). Christ, he tells us, "is the power of God and the wisdom of God" (1 Cor. 1:24). The juxtaposition of power *(dunamis)* and wisdom *(sophia)* is not coincidental here. *Sophia* is feminine and the power of *exousia* is related to a feminine consciousness.

The vocation of ordination is a call to power. But it is not the pastor's or priest's power, it is Christ's power. In at least some of the denominations surveyed in this study ordination bestows upon the recipient the power to forgive sins. It is, of course, not his or her authority, but that authority which Christ claims for the Son of Man in the Gospels: "Is it easier to say, 'Your sins are forgiven you,' or to say, 'Stand up and walk'? But to convince you that the Son of Man has the right [*exousian*, power or authority] on earth to forgive sins . . . 'I say to you, stand up, take your bed, and go home'" (Luke 5:23–24). In what way Christ identified himself with the Son of Man is widely debated, but certainly the church understood this reference to be to Christ himself.

The word the Evangelist uses for right, power, or authority to forgive sins is important. *Exousia* means literally in Greek "out of being." It is an authority or power which flows from the inside out and is grounded not in our status or role, but in our center of being, who we are. It is a power rooted in the authenticity of the person; he or she is who he or she appears to be. But such authenticity comes at a high price, as I shall insist again and again throughout this book. At the very least, it will not make us popular.

At a clergy conference typical of a number of such gatherings, I recall making the point that the spiritual life is necessarily subversive of our fondest assumptions about ourselves, and also making the additional point that the people of the church claim that they want someone of spiritual depth as their pastor. I was confronted on this with some bitterness by a priest who questioned the sincerity of people who claim they want a pastor of spiritual depth and yet act as if that is the last thing they want. He said, speaking out of experience, "If spirituality is fundamentally subversive, it will not get you elected bishop."

There are other ways to power in the church and many seek them. One of the persons interviewed, a quiet, scholarly, Roman Catholic priest, spoke sadly and yet firmly to me of his decision to avoid where possible clerical gatherings at which his bishop and the chancellor were present. The sycophancy of the clergy, he explained, left him ill and life is too short to suffer that. I have seen the same behavior toward ecclesiastical superiors at other gatherings—Episcopal, Methodist, Baptist—so no denomination has a corner on that market. Another Roman Catholic priest spoke to me of his amazement at hearing a bishop speak of himself as being "at this point in my career." What, he asked, does that mean? Is it true that if a bishop comes into a small diocese and does his work well and "keeps his nose clean" that he may advance higher? What does "higher" mean, he inquired? What has happened, he went on, to a sense of vocation?

External power comes with the acquisition of role and status. There is an interesting play on the power from within and the power that comes with rank in the story of the centurion who comes to Jesus to ask him to heal his servant (Matt. 8:5–10). The centurion uses the analogy of his own power to suggest that Jesus can heal at long distance by virtue of Jesus' power. Of course, the power is of a different kind. Jesus' is *exousia*, from the very nature of his being, while the centurion's is external.

The Greek word for this external power or authority occurs in the New Testament in its verbal form only, *authenteo*. Interestingly, it occurs only once where the author of 1 Timothy writes, "I do not permit a woman to be a teacher, nor must woman domineer *(authentein)* over man; she should be quiet" (1 Tim. 2:12). In the author's work power of this kind is given to men only. The irony is that *exousia* is the power of the feminine, coming out of receptivity and love to change a world.

Authentēo as an adjective translates "master," implying that one is to become master over another. It is society that gives such power. It is a bit like the English custom of calling a bishop "my lord," which title honors with one hand, but with the other takes away the intimate power of the spiritual guide.

One acquires external power by playing the game. The first rule is to be inoffensive and nonthreatening, because the source of external power is the system and those who manipulate the system. God help him or her who subverts the system or those in power. Systems need to maintain their equilibrium and the monitors of the system do not wish to be made uncomfortable. The election of bishops, moderators, rectors, pastors, and other church officials is a guarantee, people being what sinners we are, to assure the advancement of mediocrity and banality. It is all part of what one pastor called "power politics in the name of the Lord."

I do not believe that most persons seek ordination in order to get advancement in the church. There are career ladders with greater reward. The personality profiles I have seen only confirm the opinion that the vast majority of individuals responding to the call tend toward the end of the spectrum that holds dreamers, visionaries, and thinkers rather than the end that produces politicians, entrepreneurs, and go-getters. But they are taught that if they are to educate their children, live in reasonable comfort, maintain a car, enjoy even a modicum of the material wealth of our country, they must "pay the piper and dance to his tune." This is how the quest for external power is promoted. The lust for power never quite gets so preoccupying that in the early morning hours there is not a sinking feeling that something has been lost.

Yet it becomes all too easy to justify a ministry that regularly requires us to "belly up" to the bar at the local country club. We become a part of that ongoing power play that feeds the "messianic grandeur," as one pastor put it, that afflicts some clergy. It is difficult to discover what in this style of life fits the Gospel of Jesus Christ, but we can become inured to its judgment.

Crucifixion is no symbol of success in late-twentieth-century America. Yet, control is certainly an indication of being somebody. So there is a satisfaction in having a power over others that does not require us to face suffering, failure, and an honest appraisal of our own unworthiness, rather than the power of wisdom, which requires this and more. The professional model of ministry has encouraged us to think that this external power of control is what ministry is all about. To control our "clients," to control our "careers," to control our "certification" as professionals are all objectives in which the society persistently socializes the pastor or priest. As the centurion said of himself, "I say to one, 'Go,' and he goes; to another, 'Come here,' and he comes." Those are the words of a "professional" but have little to do with vocation.

The very thing that is true of the Gospel contradicts those who would achieve political success in the church by being inoffensive. "We proclaim Christ," says Paul, "—yes, Christ nailed to the cross . . . a stumbling block [*skandalon*] to Jews and folly to Greeks" (1 Cor. 1:23). It is the scandal of the Gospel that breaks open our presuppositions and enables us to be open to the Word of God. It is this scandal that makes the Christian faith so exciting, so different from acedia. It is to the nonthreatening, wishy-washy pastor or priest, just as to the church in Laodicea, that John the Elder wrote, "Because you are lukewarm, neither hot nor cold, I will spit you out of my mouth" (Rev. 3:16).

Insulation and Evasion

I wanted to be a priest ever since I was eleven years old. My father, who was a very devout Christian, had mixed feelings about this rather precocious ambition. In my teens he was concerned that I not get overly involved in religious activities, because, as he explained, my interest might burn out. My father's wisdom has continued to impress me as I think back on those years. I recall as a university chaplain young men or women recommended to me as hardworking church people by their pastors, inasmuch as they had been very active in high school parish groups. In time I came to expect little of such persons; most were religious burnouts at eighteen.

The problem of pastoral burnout is an important concern today in ministry studies. It can be defined as vocational exhaustion, the depletion of resources to fulfill one's responsibilities. Pastoral burnout can be faced honestly and remedial action taken, or it can be like a hidden cancer among the ordained. When admitted it is a form of battle wound, when hidden it becomes a form of acedia that manifests itself in insulation and evasion.

The sin that leads to pastoral burnout is like a two-edged sword—it cuts two ways. What gets the pastor into the problem is the temptation to evade his or her own spiritual emptiness by becoming as busy as possible. I recall a parishioner I cordially disliked: He was having marital problems and I called him and asked him if I might help. He replied that I came too late. He had asked me a month before and I had been too busy, writing a sermon. As I reflect back on that incident from the benefit of fifteen to twenty years hindsight, I realize that this man represents a piece of myself that I do not like and I do not wish to face. I was too busy to talk to him. But business for its own sake eventually results in burnout, which depletes the energy necessary to face the inner self.

One of the clergy interviewed in the research for this book described evasion as the unwillingness "to answer the phone, the door bell, and the mail." Another person suggested that clergy avoid visiting hospitals, one of the tasks they have difficulty doing. Evasion is the fear of meeting people in any way in which the priest or pastor is not in control and in which he or she may be required to give of oneself in anything but a routine manner. The inner life of the ordained person has become empty. There is nothing to give and the fear is that we will be found out.

Insulation is the careful protection of the person from any confrontation for which there is no energy. Our fantasy is that we have become extremely fragile and that our only hope is to protect ourselves. We become angry. "They" are out to get us—they being our superior, the church board, the parishioners, the community, or just about anyone. I have found myself on occasion and all too frequently I have heard clergy speaking of the people to whom they have been called to serve as the enemy. It comes out in hostile sermons, sometimes very carefully veiled, as well as in the simple avoidance of human contact.

Perhaps worse than the anger is the cynicism. Likely candidates for clerical burnout are the romantics, who believe that they possess a boundless source of love and care. What feeds this illusion is the "feeling that they [the clergy] have to be a perfect reflection of the image of God," as one person interviewed put it. I am convinced that this is no exaggeration; many priests and pastors work themselves into an impossible situation based precisely on this belief. Such attempted omnipotence, coupled with a sentimental motivation, is doomed to quick exhaustion. No one can function as a pastor who depends upon himself or herself alone. There has to be a place to feed the spirit—the caring other person and God himself. We have to risk openness to such relationship, with its accompanying confrontation and judgment, or there is no love in us.

It is just this willingness to listen that clerical cynics will not allow. They defend themselves by assuming that everyone else is like them or they are phonies. They dismiss prayer because it does not bring immediate "results," forgetting that prayer is nothing unless it demands years of disciplined waiting. Theology is ignored on the grounds that it is purposely obtuse, full of jargon, and ultimately irrelevant. Cynical pastors may well pursue the theory of the human sciences in a naive fashion, while refusing to become learned in their own discipline of theology. Such ordained persons must insulate themselves by a persistent, exhausting self-justification, because at heart their fear is that the world is not as they want it to be, a place to be their own angry, cynical selves. There is that dim intuition that if they were truly prayerful persons their self-justification would be demolished and they would once again have to become vulnerable on more than their own terms.

In classical Greek of the fifth and fourth centuries before Christ there is a word for energy, *daimōn*. It becomes personified as a divine inner presence. Socrates (c.469–399 b.c.) explains to his followers that he has found it necessary, if he is to live a good and beautiful life, to listen to his *daimon*. In this sense it is God moving within the person to unite that person to himself. It is experienced as a longing to do the good, to achieve the beautiful, and to know God. Paul speaks of this desire when he writes in praise of love, "Now we see only puzzling reflections in a mirror, but then we shall see face to face" (1 Cor. 13:12).

The Greek word *daimōn* has become our English word "demon," which is an evil spirit that destroys us. Actually it appears only once in the best texts of the New Testament: the story of the Matthean Gadarene swine. "The demons called out to him [Jesus] saying, 'If you cast us out, send us into the herd of swine'" (Matt. 8:31, translation mine). But why by this time had *daimon* taken on a negative connotation? Perhaps because we had discovered the threat of chaos and possibility of destruction to which the divine energy brings us if we are to risk attempts at union with God. We choose to play it safe.

The insulation and evasion that besets some clergy and turns them; into angry cynics is possibly the fear of their own daimonic—*not* demonic—desire driving them into the wilderness of themselves and the human community. Afraid of the source of energy, we shut ourselves off from it. A curious deception has taken place. We have labeled that best urging within ourselves as demonic and have turned from it to fall into a banal isolation that is truly demonic. Gregory of Nyssa (d. 394) wrote so long ago, "For this demon who does men harm and corrupts them is intensely concerned that his subjects not look to heaven but that they stoop to earth and make bricks within themselves out of clay."[2]

The Confusion of Means and Ends

One of the pastors who helped in the preparation for this book told a story about Rufus Jones (1863–1948), a member of the Society of Friends, for many years a professor of philosophy at Haverford College, and a man of deep spiritual commitment. Jones returned home after studying in Europe and attended the local Quaker meeting. When he felt moved by the Spirit to speak, Jones shared what was very erudite discourse. When he finished there was a silence, and then an elderly lady commented, "I know in the Bible Jesus tells us to feed his sheep. He even tells us to feed his lambs." She paused, "But nowhere can I recall that he tells us to feed his giraffes."

This pastor's point was that one of the sins of clergy is to make communication impossible by talking at a level that only a seminary graduate can understand. I do not altogether agree with his belief that everything should be kept simple, perhaps at the level of story, because there are things that need to be thought and said that can only be expressed in a technical and precise language. People do have a responsibility to stretch their God-given minds. The fear of the intellectual can be a form of insulation and evasion. Yet there is an infatuation with our own words and ideas that is illustrative of the confusion of means with ends.

Ideas can become disembodied and unrelated. In this way a fundamental fear of the pastor is met: the fear of becoming vulnerable to himself or herself and to the people he or she serves. The spiritual guide must combine faith and vulnerability if he or she is to be an effective instrument. Vulnerability is a fundamental problem when one is looking for protection from the dark feelings about the self. Words become a smokescreen. My experience in attempting to pierce that veil of verbiage is that I am met with indignation. No gentleman, it would seem, would "undress" the other in this manner.

But let me speak of myself. My own experience is that when my words are unrelated to my concept of myself and I am challenged, I become angry. Upon reflection it seems to me that I am afraid I have been caught in a lie. It is not that I do not believe in my head what I am saying, but there is a contradiction between what I am saying and how I think I am. I experience the other person as a judge too close to the truth. They have revealed not so much to others but to me that "the emperor has no clothes." What I need to remember is that the judge is within myself.

The alternative to anger is to understand that words are means to self-awareness and communication of self and to admit that they bear an inadequate, yet necessary, relationship to the experience of being loved by God. God does not love me because "I have it all together." I do not earn his love because as a priest I share with others a consistent system of thought, expressing a totally congruent self. I come to God as a child, and it is all right to feel as a child in the presence of others whom I perceive as seeing through my verbiage to the real me.

A friend who spends a good part of his ministry working with pastors, focusing on their spiritual lives, described how he sees this intellectual distancing taking place. In his conferences, which require a deep journey within the self, clergy will want to talk about Jungian archetypes or some equivalent conceptual framework and resist all his efforts to bring the discussion back to themselves. They will strive to keep the conversations "out there" where it is more comfortable. The discussion of the mandala—a quartered circle, an archetype of the self—is a great deal safer, for example, than sharing the dark corners of our own soul.

Abstraction is not the only use of words that thwarts the spiritual instrumentality of the pastor, however. More subtle is the "cracker barrel philosophy" of the pastor who poses as a person of the people. The misleading aphorisms of popular religion often hide the ambiguities of sin and the human quest for God. The "simple religion of Jesus" is not so simple because human beings are very complex, and we need to be challenged to deal with our strangeness.

Think of the tyranny of the "practical religion," preached by some contemporaries, which promises success as measured by our culture. What does it say to those who try hard and fail? Think of the cruel manipulation of our affect, which requires the emotional cripple to look to the church each Sunday for a "fix" to make it through the week. What happens when it no longer works? Think of the reduction of sin to passion, leaving us moral retardates. What happens to those who are crushed by the injustice and oppression of the righteous?

Another way in which means and ends are confused is by "playing church." I ran into a former student of mine in an airport. We had the expected conversation; we talked about his classmates who were my students. He mentioned each student by the title of "Father." I have no objection to that title when it means something, but we were talking about people who will always be to me friends, if not my students. We discussed who was doing well and who was doing not so well. His measure of success was the priest's ability to embody a model of priesthood that he (incorrectly) identified with the English Tractarians of the mid-nineteenth century. I was amazed to discover that he carried in his pocket copies of last year's parish report complete with the statistics of success. The thought occurred to me as we talked that if I dropped dead in that airport in the next thirty minutes, I hoped to heaven that he was not around. This was not someone, I thought, who would understand what it means to die!

Objects, material things are important in religion. Someone asked me once what I thought of the Shroud of Turin. The fact is that I do not think about the Shroud of Turin, but I can understand why someone might. I am fond of the story of Louis Duchesne (1843–1922), a

French church historian, discovered by a student kneeling before a relic of the true cross that he had proved to be a fraud. His explanation of his behavior was that the relic was at least a thousand years old. Reverence is appropriate in the presence of any object, event, or person hallowed by the countless prayers and pious hopes of the people of God. Such things can have a way of leading anyone with sensitivity into the depths of the human spiritual experience, much as the portrait of my mother on our mantle, made at age eight just before she left Scotland to emigrate to Canada, draws me into a reverie fraught with lights and shadows.

But the ecclesiastical dilettante makes the things of religion—the vestments, the limp leather Bible, the massed choirs, the organ, the stained glass windows—into an end. He or she refuses to deal with what lies beyond the objects and sanctifies them: the rejoicing, the mourning, the fear, the desire, and the true hope of which these appearances are a promise are all avoided. Things become the smokescreen for a hollow life that the ordained is certain God cannot accept, much less use.

The answer to the dilettante is not, however, an acerbic, secular rationalism. The priest or pastor who expresses his contempt for piety by embracing the latest fashion of the human sciences in lieu of a spiritual theology is equally transparent as those he would despise.

Nancy Van Scoyoc in *Women, Change, and the Church*[3] tells a moving story of a woman who experienced a sudden remission of a rare disease. This healing was a profound spiritual experience. Although she tried, she could not bring herself to tell her pastor of this experience. Why? My experience as a priest who serves as the dean of a seminary is that many students who have had religious experiences have to test me in several ways before they will speak of these strange events. Their experience has been that clergy dismiss the transcendent possibilities and offer glib secular explanations for what has happened. I recall a television series on religion in America where a woman described how for all her adult life her preacher had told the congregation to experience God. When she did and told him about it, he gave her the name of a psychiatrist with the suggestion that she needed to talk to him.

Sometimes the persons most ready to listen and entertain the validity of genuine religious experience are those trained in the so-called secular disciplines, which some clergy use to escape their own vocation. There is great value in the human sciences for spiritual theology. They provide ample means to further the Gospel's end. It is only when they

are used to provide a defense against the risk of spiritual instrumentality that they become a problem to the church and a sin of the clergy.

Another form of confusing means with ends is to commit ourselves
to all kinds of means that obscure the ends. As one person described it:

> Most clergy do this by default because they don't know what
> the hell else to do . . . When people come to the clergy person
> and really want to grow, the clergy person has no idea what to
> do. Because of that they give him a lot of garbage, usually in
> the form of books. And most of the time they are books that
> the people can't understand.

An endless variety of means becomes a good way of assuring that what
we do never has to be evaluated. We never get to a point where we arrive at the goal we profess or know that we will not arrive. We are always in the process of getting started.

There is a truth in spiritual theology that perfection lies in the purity of the process, but there is nothing pure about garbage. It is indicative, rather, of a failure of pastors to work for simplicity of life so
that they can share what works for them without troubling the inquirer with all the other stuff.

The Fear of Failure

At the root of acedia and clerical sins of un-passion lies the fear of
failure.

It has become the practice in some dioceses within the Episcopal
Church to interview a selected group of priests who are willing to be
nominated for bishop in that diocese. In one such selection process a
question was asked of the candidates: "How do you handle failure?"
One man, a demonstrably successful cardinal rector, probably lost the
election on the basis of his answer to that question alone, which was "I
don't recall ever having failed."

How can we serve a Lord, the symbol of whose failure is above
our altars, on top of our churches, on our stationery, and around our
necks, and claim to be a stranger to failure? The power of Christ's Passion is that every human being can identify with it, if he or she just
gives it some thought. Despite our best intentions and our fervent

hopes, each of us is nailed to his or her cross daily. Certainly this is true of the ordained person, who is called to be "another Christ" and to risk living by values that the world not only rejects but perceives as subversive of its goals and objectives.

In interviewing persons for this study I noticed something curious about reactions to the question of what failure means in their spiritual life. It was one of the two questions—the other had to do with sexuality—of which they frequently wanted clarification. I myself have found this section difficult to write. I think back over my own twenty-seven years as an ordained priest and I realize that I left one place to go to another saying that the job I came to do I had done. But what if I have to leave a place having failed? What do I make of that? I simply prefer not to think about it.

There were notable exceptions to this resistance to failure. One priest spoke to the issue quite eloquently, "It can be," he said, "an excellent runway for the plane [of spiritual growth] to take off on . . ." In the American society failure is taboo, so we cover everything up, including death, "because I think we regard death as the supreme failure." Death in all its forms is looked upon as failure and failure is to be avoided at all costs. But the spiritual life is an act of dying to self.

It has become almost a cliché that the ordained person is not called to be successful, but to be faithful. Fidelity requires above all an openness that leaves us terribly vulnerable. Every effort to protect that vulnerability requires us to deny our vocation. Consequently we are called to bear within ourselves the failure of the world to subsist on its own and to carry within ourselves the pain of the cross, even the death of God's son.

A faithful priest spoke to me a day or so after the death of a friend. As he put it, there was no person in this world to whom he was closer. At age forty-two one Saturday afternoon his friend dropped dead without warning, leaving his wife and two teenage children. The priest had rushed to the hospital only to be there in time to assist at the last rites. Then he dissolved into the arms of his friend's wife and with her wept like a baby. Had he failed, he asked me? No, he had celebrated the failure of life as only a priest could, in mourning and in hope.

It is the fear of celebrating the world's failure—ourselves included—that leaves clergy persons in their cold sins. We are in fact called to be magnificent failures, for which only the dying will give us thanks.

Extramarital Genital Relationships

Ask a priest or pastor about what constitutes temptation for the clergy and almost without fail sex is mentioned. It is a common topic of conversation at clergy gatherings. I have given it the clinical-sounding title "extramarital genital relationships" because I want to distinguish this specific kind of physical relationship from other kinds of relationships, all of which are in some sense sexual. Furthermore, I would discourage the titillation that comes with contemplating the "fallen priest" by giving the sin a thoroughly dispassionate name.

The vulnerability of the good pastor leads to sexual intercourse more often than probably many people realize. The clear impression from the interviews is that the temptation is there every day and it is a difficult struggle. One pastor, to quote him exactly, said, "Sexual [sin] is probably as great a temptation of the clergy as most are incapable of dealing with." I assume he meant that many ordained persons do succumb from time to time in spite of efforts to the contrary.

The fact that the extramarital relations of the clergy both create such a scandal and make such popular reading is more a comment on the public image of the priest or pastor than it is an evaluation of the malign nature of this sin. The sins already discussed in this chapter are more devastating by nature than the frailty of clerical flesh. In a moralistic society we are blind to the reality of gross sin and are inclined to express horror at what stirs deeply and what we envy and yet fear. Scratch the rigid moralist and you often find one deeply attracted to the illicitly sexual.

Never was this more evident to me than when someone showed me a number of comic books published by a fundamentalist group in the revivalist tradition. Aside from the caricatures of those with whom they disagreed—Roman Catholics, biblical scholars, anthropologists, theologians—as degenerates or "wimps," this material designed for adults and teenagers was filled with violence and had strong sexual undertones. Pictures of torture chambers, with nuns presiding over the rack or hook, appeal to the prurient interests of the reader far more than *Playboy* or *Penthouse*. It was grossly obscene.

I recently heard of a pastor who had been found to have had genital relations with seventeen women in his parish. The very report evokes a number of thoughts, not excluding the suspicion of satyriasis. One would hope that instead of figuratively burning him at the stake, someone might have asked him what he learned out of this experience, because there was a great deal to be learned there. But in our horror we so often never ask.

Which is to say that the sexual sin of the clergy figures prominently not so much because of the act itself, but because of what we make of that act . . . or do not make of it.

Conclusion

I recall when I was a little boy and went to movies there was usually a cartoon. Not infrequently the cartoon was about the struggle of Donald Duck or some other character caught between good and evil. On one shoulder would be Donald Duck done up as an angel and on the other shoulder Donald Duck garbed as a devil. The two would argue over his will.

It was a common belief in the early church that God gives each of us an angel "to help in the life of each person" and a demon "who afflicts the life of man and contrives against our nature."[4] It would follow from this that the inner journey is just like the trip into the desert. It is a place where we must fight the demon and find the angel. Pastors or priests are ones who know this and do this as their vocation, with no need to justify their existence on any other grounds.

II. The Character

4. Obeying the Inner Intention

DISCIPLINE and obedience are not popular words among many clergy, yet both lie at the heart of the spiritual journey and the Christian life. Tilden Edwards, Director of the Shalem Institute in Washington, D. C., and a noted spiritual theologian, says that discipline is what allows attention to the truth of God in life.

Obedience is one of the evangelical counsels, the three traditional gospel principles that were made popular in the monastic movement and other forms of the religious life in Christianity. They were derived from the story of the man from the ruling class, who comes to Jesus and asks him, "Good Master, what must I do to win eternal life?" After a preliminary inquiry, Jesus comes to the nub of the matter: "Sell everything you have and distribute to the poor . . . and come, follow me." Peter reports that the apostles have done all this and Jesus enigmatically replies, "There is no one who has given up home, or wife . . . for the sake of the kingdom of God, who will not be repaid many times over" (Luke 18:18–30). Out of this passage comes the call to live a life of poverty, chastity, and obedience.

There is no doubt that in repudiating the religious life as a legitimate form of Christian witness or in concluding it is not their particular vocation many ordained persons lift from themselves the challenge of the gospel admonition. Of course, the Evangelist did not have in mind a class of specialists in spiritual matters or even the religious orders, no matter what we may think of them; he had in mind the disciples of Jesus the Christ—you and me. We cannot escape what he says too easily. If it is true, as one person interviewed suggests, that the ordained person has the responsibility "to run a little faster than all the crowd to climb the tree to see the Lord," then we need to understand what poverty, chastity, and obedience mean for ourselves.

This chapter is about obedience or discipline. If we can exclude our unpleasant associations with the word discipline, it is helpful to remember that it comes from the Latin, *disciplina*, which means "teaching." It is related to *discipulus*, which is the Latin translation of the Greek word very common in the New Testament, *mathetes*, meaning "disciple." A disciple is one who follows the discipline of his master. This is what it is to be a follower of Jesus Christ.

The problem comes when we ask ourselves who or what enforces the discipline of Jesus Christ. The obvious abuse of this by church people, by parents, and by others in authority creates sufficient confusion that there is cause for the excuse that to be undisciplined is preferable to living under tyranny. The common observation of everyone I interviewed is that the clergy as a group are, on the whole, tragically undisciplined. It is cold comfort to remind ourselves that this has been the charge, throughout the history of the church, but it is no less a scandal for its ubiquity.

The Internal Intention

Spiritual discipline begins with our ability to listen attentively to our internal intention. The common Greek verb in the New Testament for "obey" is *hupakouō*, which has the technical meaning of what the doorkeeper in the ancient world did. He listened for a knock at the outside door and admitted those who were entitled to enter. The doorkeeper was of course a slave. The word has the meaning of the manner in which a slave listened to his master. Consequently, the image is of a patient, attentive, and respectful waiting of the disciple for the teaching of the master.

The enemy of attentive listening is extraneous noise, both the externally generated and the internally generated kinds. I am writing this book in a cottage in the mountains of western North Carolina. The cottage is in a little valley at the bottom of a winding drive and some two hundred yards from a county dirt road. The nearest house is a quarter of a mile away. There is so little noise reaching me that the sound of a car on the road above demands my attention. I am aware in contrast of the constant noise that generally clutters our hearing.

To many, noise is the merciful, meaningless babble that shuts out the accusing inner voices. In June, 1980, I was invited to speak in London, Ontario, where my maternal grandparents are buried, where my mother grew up, where my father came as a penniless professor to court her, and where I came as a child with my sisters to visit my loving Granny and Grandpa. The night of my visit I lay in the guest suite, far removed from all sound of human habitation, and tossed and turned. The quiet was strangely painful. In the silence I heard the voices of my grandparents and my parents, crying, laughing, making love, struggling to make themselves heard, but for no apparent purpose. It was part of me and inside me and there was no resolution. I looked for a radio to turn on and longed for the voices of people outside my room to shut out the inner voices.

Many persons ordained or not, live in a fairly constant state of noise, with their unresolved past and the uncertain present breaking in on them. They lack a still center and it is only from such a quiet point that we can listen attentively. When I was in my first parish, which was located in the middle of the city, a constant stream of indigents came through. One came into my office and wanted to tell me his story. I sat as if to listen but was deeply troubled inside over some issue now long forgotten. I remember I was fiddling with a pencil. The man stopped his story, looked at me and said, "Young Father, the least you can do is listen." He was right. There was no still center in me.

Thomas Merton (1915–1968), the fascinating Cistercian monk whose writings continue to increase in popularity, found the busy life of a Trappist very disconcerting. Despite the fact that speaking is severely curtailed in a Cistercian monastery, he found the place incredibly noisy. For many years he sought permission to live as a hermit on the property of the monastery. He needed the quiet that he might listen. Too frequently we do not understand the hermit's discipline, a discipline that needs to be ours in spirit, if not in fact.

The listening to which I refer is one that is unfocused, yet directed within the person. It is an intuitive hearing or felt thinking. It is the "penetrating and free gaze of the soul extended everywhere in perceiving things"[1] which Richard of St. Victor identifies with contemplation. This has been called tacit knowing, as compared with explicit acts of knowing. Tacit knowing is analogous to seeing something out of the corner of our eye that we could not see if we looked straight ahead. We have all had this experience. Gazing at the stars we see a star in our peripheral vision that disappears when we turn to look for it. Looking at a landscape, we see a movement off to one side that vanishes as we turn our head. It is akin to struggling to balance a checkbook late into the evening, only to discover the mistake in the first five minutes of work on it the next morning.

Psychotherapists have sometimes called this "listening with the third ear," by which they mean attending to what is going on inside oneself-as-therapist during the interaction with the client. It bears a relationship to the tradition that the shaman, the religious adept of hunting and gathering cultures, had a third eye, located between the customary two, by which he could see inside the soul of another. The anatomical images point to the intuition that somewhere within ourselves is a congruence of consciousness with those with whom we are related. The inner self becomes the source of openness to meaning.

H. A. Williams, a member of the English Community of the Resurrection, writes, "Fundamentally obedience consists of discovering what you most truly and deeply are or, better, what you have it in you to be, and in being loyal to the insight you have thus received."[2] One does this by attentive listening and what is discovered is *the content of that structure of meaning with which one engages the world*. This is what I mean by *intention*.

There are many ways of describing who we are. At the source of our being human, however, is that reality that lies embedded in our minds in the form of a constellation of images. From that constellation are constructed by each of us the metaphors, the stories, the rituals, the models by which the world and our place in it are defined and our actions determined. Whereas every form of psychotherapy ultimately works on this principle in some way, there is a school related to family therapy that speaks of metaphor transplants. If that constellation of images is such that the human action that it provokes is perceived as destructive, the solution is to replace it with a healthier metaphor.

There is an assumption here about the cognitive process, that is, what it is we know when we say we know, that may need explanation. One way of getting at this is to ask what we mean by the "real world." "He needs to enter the 'real world,'" I have heard it said. Reality is not something "out there" that the mind absorbs; and reality is not something implanted in the mind independent of the "out there." Reality is what the subject makes of his or her experience of the objective world by means of language—the images embedded in the mind. Everyone has "real world," so the problem is not "entering" some universally apparent reality, but in *relating* multiple realities.

In a sense life is the performance of our perceived reality. Life at a minimum is a living out of an endless series of vignettes, played by the various personifications of ourself on the stage of our psychic land-scape, that is, the topography of our memory. To personify in this sense is to hold within our memory a cast of characters who embody those values we hold dear. For example, nurturing becomes the Mother, overcoming evil becomes the Hero, and understanding becomes the Sage. We live out the vignettes of Mother, Hero, and Sage, often in mini-performances unrelated to one another.

One can hope for a consistent story line that runs through each person's life, tying the various vignettes together. When such a general plot exists the internal intention of a person has a perceptible direc-tion and purpose. He or she may report what he is doing and what he chooses not to do. A sense of contentment is present and this sense of contentment appeared to be characteristic of the subjects in this study. Inasmuch as such centering is at least partially a function of age, it is not surprising most of those interviewed were over forty.

In working with these clergy, however, it was very difficult for them to grasp the concept of life as performance. The temptation to project our internal intention on the world and assume that this is re-ality appears to be almost overwhelming. This projection in its most destructive form is called fideism and is characteristic of biblical and doctrinal literalism. Fideism and literalism were not problems for the men and women I interviewed. But it was difficult for them to look at their actions and then move within to identify those images of self that shaped those actions. We are not generally conscious of the metaphor-ical nature of reality as we constitute it.

If there is an exception to this difficulty, it lies among the few women in the sample. This is probably a result of their struggle to be-come what has been the exclusive role of men, as well as their sensi-tivity to the projections of the people in their churches upon them. Women clergy are forced to be aware of the metaphors—new and old—of the priest or pastor and have to relate these to their own self-images and the internal intention in which they are embedded.

Cognitive theory is often difficult to grasp, but it is important that the reader understand my argument, because there is a clear, implicit criticism in it of the model in which almost all of us have been falsely socialized and that makes spiritual discipline appear nonsense. I am re-ferring to positivism or scientism, which claims that things are only as they appear to our senses. It is the mechanistic model of humankind that must be toppled, if we are to understand that spiritual discipline is an attending to the center of our humanity, the internal intention shaped by God.

Years ago I was a "front man" for Milwaukee Planned Parenthood. I looked safe in my black suit and round collar, talking about sex before audiences that included people who thought coitus was a subhuman activity. However, this role threw me in with people who often talked in a language alien to my own. On the occasion of one speech I mentioned that we must attend carefully to what we make of our sexuality, because "sex is among the most powerful symbols we have." I was followed by a speaker who was a professor of marriage and family. He thanked the "reverend" for his "inspiring message," and then averred, "Sex is not only a powerful symbol, it is real."

The question is: What is real if not a powerful symbol or image? The professor had totally missed the point. (He told me later that he had once tried reading Kant, but gave up on him. More's the pity!) Either we are automatons who "screw," or we are human beings for whom sexual images are the core of our reality in a world of other humans. There is no in-between. If reality is not symbolic, it is not worth talking about, much less knowing. And the tragedy is that even some of us, the ordained, are not altogether clear about this.

Discovering who we most truly and deeply are, as H. A. Williams challenges us to do, consists in identifying those images and their relationships that constitute our internal structure of meaning. There is in that intentional structure a promise of the future, as he goes on to say. We are goal-oriented creatures. Each of us has a history: a past, a present, and the freedom to pursue a future. It is within that history that we as Christians believe that God speaks. God is the God of history. "Then he who sat on the throne said, 'Behold! I am making all things new! . . . I am the Alpha and the Omega, the beginning and the end'" (Rev. 21:5–6).

What I have said is consistent with the intuition of Christian masters through the centuries. Of course, Julian of Norwich was neither a transcendental Thomist nor an existential phenomenologist, but her observation is important:

> But our passing life which we have here does not know in our senses what our self is, but we know in our faith. And when we know and see, truly and clearly, what our self is, then we shall truly and clearly see and know our Lord God in the fulness of joy.[3]

The Sources of Images

I asked those interviewed to describe turning points in their spiritual journey. One priest spoke of the serious illness of his wife at a time when he was pursuing a secular career. Faced for the first time with a problem he could not overcome, he and his wife were led to join a charismatic prayer group. It was at this time that the person of God in an intimate way, he said, "really came in my life . . . through a series of encounters with individuals." First there was the wife of a co-worker who told her story and then there were a number of persons in an organization that taught and practiced spiritual healing. In the meanwhile his wife experienced a dramatic, instantaneous healing, which was verified by the doctors. "It was," as he said, "astounding."

We are often wont to say that we find God or Christ in others. This assertion appears to contradict my point that obedience and spiritual discipline begin with an attention to the inner self. But in fact it does not contradict it. For the significance of any image, no matter what its source, lies in what it does for *our perception of ourself* in relation to our experience of the world.

The key to the account of this priest's discovery of an intimate personal relation to God lay in the crisis of his wife's illness, the first problem in his life he could not overcome by trying hard. The effect of that kind of crisis is to crack open our presuppositions about the world and to force us to look deeper *within ourselves* for the world's meaning. There is a profound sense in which on such occasions we go to the bottom within ourselves. In these circumstances we carry with us resources that we intuitively know will provide images that can illumine those dark depths.

Perhaps this is why thousands of people looked at Jesus of Nazareth and saw the deranged son of a carpenter and a dozen or so looked at him and saw the Son of God. The latter were in some inchoate way—the Gospels say they were as little children—willing to look deep within and let Jesus illumine their lives. As the two disciples who met the risen Lord on the road to Emmaus said, "Did we not feel our hearts on fire as he talked with us on the road and explained the scriptures to us?" (Luke 24:32). The biblical term "heart" here is very close to what I mean by internal intention.

Those images that form and illumine the internal intention lead us to a personal knowledge of God, who is operant within us. They constitute the substance of the fundamental self. The cipher of being becomes palpable as it takes on images that give it essence or "whole-ness." Those images can come from many sources, but there are three particular areas that inform the Christian disciple.

First, there is the source we have already mentioned, the explicit or implicit witness of others. The priest of whom I have written in this section referred to the wife of the co-worker. She had phoned him and said, "I must speak with you. The strangest thing has happened to me." She had gone to a New Year's Eve party to find instead a prayer group, at which she discovered her need to reach out to this man, now ordained. This was an explicit witness. But another person I inter-viewed described the implicit, yet equally powerful, example of his parents, who in his presence lived a Christian life.

In what is now a classical illustration, Dante (1265–1321) de-scribed his experience of the young girl, Beatrice, whom he saw only on a couple of occasions, but who was for him a true *theotokos*, "god-bearer." Speaking personally, there is to me one who is indeed a *theotokos*, in a very subtle and mysterious way, one from whom I re-ceive images that illumine my own inner life in ways that draw me be-yond myself to know God. This corresponds to a more general observation that in the lives of the spiritually mature, models, or other persons who form and illumine their lives, seem to be important.

Spiritual discipline requires that we seek to be receptive to the relationship between the questions that arise within our own inner self and the images that present themselves in the lives of others. A serious illness is obviously a question provoker. But any awareness of our own finitude and contingency is equally capable of raising such issues as can be informed by the Christlike lives of others. I reflect on my "Beatrice" and as a result I contemplate my own death as a barbed gift, for she has spoken much to me of the meaning of death for her.

Second, there is the source of the written word in the Bible and subsequent texts. The priest who spoke to me of his wife's healing went on to say of his pilgrimage:

> Curiosity on my part and spiritual hunger led me on. And so over the next year, I would say—it was probably the year of greatest spiritual growth in my life—I had an insatiable desire to learn what the Bible said. I'd read it off and on, but I sat down and I outlined the entire Bible. I really learned it . . . I've used that stuff ever since.

The medieval church taught that spiritual discipline consisted of *lectio, meditatio, oratio*, "reading, reflection, prayer." Henri Nouwen in his book *Reaching Out*[4] speaks of words, silence, and guidance. There was no question in any of those persons I consulted about the absolute centrality of the Scriptures to spiritual growth.

The point is, however, not to read the Bible as an object of study, but to incorporate the scriptural images into the heart. When I was in seminary the chaplain was fond of reminding us that the mind is the color of its thoughts. For this reason, he explained, we should become saturated with the words of the Scriptures so that its images fill our thoughts. It is not a matter of proving anything from the Bible, but it is an issue of learning in an oblique fashion to shape one's world in the language of God's word. It is in this way that our outlook on the world is scriptural, we come to pray the Scriptures, and we pray without ceasing.

If this is hard for us to do today, it is because we read the Bible as if it were a guidebook. An Old Testament scholar of my acquaintance once built a model of the Jewish Temple according to the measurements in Ezekiel. The model collapsed. As he pointed out, the Bible is not a specification book for the architectural engineering of Jewish temples. The Bible is poetry and needs to be read as poetry. It evokes the right questions, hints at the answers, and leaves us sustained to walk into the mystery itself. This is why it is essential to our spiritual discipline. It is a companion on the quest.

To a lesser degree this is true of other Christian texts. The lives of the saints, the canons of the councils, the speculations of the theologians, and the writings of the spiritual masters are all to be chewed on. But we are not engaged in a contest to see how much new material we can read. Rereading and careful pondering is the style of the person who wishes to feed the intention of his or her being with the imagery of our Christian heritage.

Third, there is the source of our own spontaneous imagery, rising up from our unconscious and leading us back into the self to discover God. My discovery is that this is a source difficult for the research sample to affirm. Only 56 percent (nine out of sixteen) allowed the possibility that dreams might reveal the will of God, even on rare occasions, and there was small evidence of an outlook—what James Hopewell of Emory University would call "gnostic"—that would entertain the possibility of the power of such internal imagery. I think this is to be regretted.

Whatever may be the ultimate source—family rearing, genetic coding, or God—there are spontaneous images that come into our consciousness one way or another. We can be driving down the interstate, defecating, sleeping, hiking, or meditating (particularly if it is an apophatic form of meditation) when they happen. We need to be aware of them as they present themselves for our attention for what they may tell us about ourselves and, consequently, God.

These images can serve as psychopomps. The word comes from *psuchē*, meaning "soul," and *pompē*, meaning a "solemn procession, escort." Hermes was a psychopomp. So also was Charon, who in Greek mythology was the one who rowed the deceased across the River Styx to the underworld. The angelic messengers in the Scriptures are forms of psychopomps.

I have a recurring dream of a "nerd," an obnoxious, incompetent, inept, gross individual. He has no flare, no wit, no style. Sometimes I am aware in my dreams that he is a "nerd" because I know his name and that person to me is a "nerd." Sometimes it is because he is dressed like a "nerd"—trousers with suspenders, wearing only an undershirt, with a can of beer in his hand. The "nerd" in me leads me back into that shadow world behind my contempt to where God somehow cares for me despite the fact that I have failed to live up to my aspirations of perfection. God is in the garbage of my life just as much as in the competence in a way that I particularly need to appropriate. The image of the "nerd" is for me a psychopomp.

Spiritual discipline requires that we be attentive to the images that spring up into our consciousness when we least expect them, sometimes when we least want them. It takes a long period of attentive listening and a willingness to endure the pain.

Communal Obedience

Historically obedience and discipline have been viewed as imposed by the church. The classical manuals of ascetical theology in the Roman Catholic Church have defined obedience as a relationship to the hierarchy that is justified by virtue of the act itself and not any extrinsic end. In the Protestant traditions the authority of the Scriptures has demanded absolute obedience. For example, the Ten Commandments have been seen as a clear, uncompromised injunction laid upon us all.

Obedience in contemporary spiritual theology is obedience to what we are. To the extent that we saw ourselves as *simply* children of the church and/or her Scriptures, then the unqualified notion of obedience as located in external authority made sense. But this requires an understanding of the church or the Bible as a monolithic unchanging authority, which in fact neither is. We are the church, and yet the church is many things and we are more than all those things.

One person interviewed, who works full-time in the spiritual guidance of clergy and laity, spoke to this point.

> We are in such a fragmented cultural and religious situation that there is no coherent practice of the faith possible unless you are a credible rigid sectarian. The result is that you are always dealing with bits and pieces. That affects the problem of spiritual maturation today, because there is so much difficulty to trust a given place long enough—so many temptations in "the big cafeteria" around, and some of those contradict what you are doing. The result is a kind of wobbliness.

Perhaps "wobbliness" is a strong word for what was observed in this study among the clergy, but it is not too far off the target. In the research there was an acknowledgment by the respondents that the church is necessary or, at least, important. Within this general principle, however, the viewpoints varied. One man said, "If it isn't of the church, I am very leery and worried about it," but he had come to this conviction from a history of being anti-institutional. Perhaps more typical was the observation that the institutional church is to be valued "*slightly* to the positive side of neutral." Another said that he "tends to ignore it [the institutional church]." One pastor, who professed to being still as anti-institutional as anyone, admitted that a mature spirituality may well be rooted in the church, but said, "I have known one or two people who were profoundly Christian, profoundly spiritual indeed, and have in their life and ministry had minimal contact with the Christian church as such." Another one expressed the belief, "The church is divine in essence . . . but very human in her process." He went on to speak in an earthy way of his refusal to play up to the hierarchy, but added in a prayerful tone that the church is "the mystical image of God's divinity and transcendence."

I get the sense that the church is for these persons above all the people of God, the folk with whom they worship and to whom they preach and serve as pastor. The structures command their obedience in a less than compelling manner, even if they are Roman Catholic or Episcopalian. One pastor mentioned his surprise that the judicatory head described him as "spiritually mature," for he had the feeling the man hardly knew he existed. He was not alone in these feelings. There is a consistent implication that those in power in the church do not share the same concerns as they do.

There is no doubt that the pluralistic nature of our society has contributed to a diffusion of a sense of the church's claim upon the clergy. There is an almost functional congregationalism in many of these persons. They are loyal—obedient would be the wrong word—to the people they serve. A high-school administrator spoke with concern and yet great affection for the teenagers to whom he ministers. Another pastor professed his belief that God wants all people to be saved, which he learned while working among some very deprived people.

But for most of the sample their first obedience seemed to be to their inner intention. As I struggle with this question the suggestion occurs to me that there may well be fundamentally different kinds of people that make up the church. The ancient Gnostics said there were three kinds of people—*pneumatikon, psuchikon,* and *hulikon* ("spirit-like, soul-like, and stuff-like")—and I am not so sure that they did not have the seed of an important idea there. I am not reverting to some ancient fantastic cosmology or ontology that sets forth three "species" of human being. I agree with the pastor who says God wants everyone to be saved, however we interpret that. But it becomes a possibility that individuals function in different ways: some have to be coerced, some have to be active in the ecclesial system, and others, including the majority of these persons interviewed, have the ability to listen attentively to the God who speaks through their own inner intentions.

Even those who choose to obey the church—say the daily office, recite the rosary, read their Bibles regularly—do so knowing that there are other options and if they choose them they will not "go to hell." There has to be, as far as they are concerned, a personal initiative in which they affirm their freedom. The discovery of one's own freedom is a part of becoming spiritually mature. Like little children, they have to experience saying no, before they can in fact say yes.

The church in this way becomes the concrete expression of what we know is universally true; namely, we must be loyal to what is beyond the self. The Gospel is the burden of a people, not just individuals, and our fidelity to the Gospel lies in our collaborative search and sharing of values. How this particularly differs from the obedience to authority in past centuries is that our loyalty to the church expresses itself dialogically. Each person is an active agent in that quest for spiritual growth, rather than an inert recipient of the church's wisdom.

The dialogue with the church requires, however, a kind of obedience that is more profound and complex than a simple acceptance of the *magisterium* of the church for its own sake. It is such an obedience that seems to come with great difficulty to contemporary clergy. If Tilden Edwards is right and the disciplined life is that which "allows attention to the truth of God in life," then we have to commit ourselves to whatever is required to discover truth. What is required is a love of orthodoxy, but what I mean by orthodoxy is not a static something as much as it is the dynamic process of right thinking. It is here that I felt most of those interviewed lacked a desirable competence.

Inasmuch as the church is fragmented, right thinking is really the only choice if we are to avoid a solipsistic fideism, positing as eternal truth our ill-defined feelings of good will. The hermeneutic process calls for a disciplined method of relating the texts of the Christian tradition to the data of our contemporary experience. The pastor or priest or hermeneut cannot settle for notions of truth that are nothing more than a montage of emotions clothed in the garments of the tradition. This is in the final analysis dishonest. It fails to take into account the self-evident, radical shift in the understanding of human knowing that has transpired over the last two hundred years.

We know today that to know anything we begin with the human person as a historical, linguistic creature, who may use the power of language responsibly or irresponsibly. It is an irresponsible use of language to lump moral issues such as artificial contraception, abortion, divorce and remarriage, and premarital coitus under the same ethical category because they all relate to the family and condemn or approve them all unilaterally. It is an irresponsible use of language to use the Revelation of John the Elder to predict coming events in the late twentieth century, or to imply that a dogma written in Greek in the fifth century means the same thing in an English translation of the same in the late twentieth century. It is an irresponsible use of language to suggest that to love someone means I have to approve of that person's actions or that everyone has a right to happiness as they conceive it. It is an irresponsible use of language to pray contrary to the experience of space and time, as in intercessions that imply the undoing of the past ("God grant that Tom, who drove a car into a tree at seventy miles an

hour ten minutes ago, is not hurt") or contrary to the universal expectations of the future ("O Lord, may Sue not die—now or ever").

What should concern us in the disciplined life is the discovery that
those spiritually sensitive clergy interviewed in this study have a certain
tendency to minimize the need to think rightly and to use language responsibly. There were notable exceptions but the widespread problem
is evident in their inability to clarify the content of their internal intention and to grapple with the process from the construction of reality to
the decision to act. As a result their spirituality lacks a conceptual
mooring. Granted that spirituality has always been indifferent if not
hostile to theology, I do not think in the episodic world of the contemporary church we can afford this lack of obedience to right thinking. To
do so means that we become inattentive to the truth of God in life.

At the heart of the spiritual life is the attention to the cognitive
process. What is it to know? What are we doing when we are knowing?
What is it we know? These are not questions for teachers of philosophy alone. They are issues for the spiritual discipline of the priest or
pastor who would be a competent hermeneut, an instrument of the
spiritual growth of the people he serves. Julian of Norwich writes,
"Our faith comes from the natural love of our soul, and from the clear
light of our reason, and from the steadfast memory which we have
from God in our first creation."[5] It would be well for us to cultivate
"the clear light of our reason."

Conclusion

The disciplined life or obedience is not obsolete for our times, but it
takes on a very different meaning than a blind submission to external
authority. It turns inward. That inward turning is not so much to our
feelings as to our memory, understanding, and will. By memory I
mean the images that make up the structures of meaning within us
and in terms of which we see the world. Understanding here is the
ability to illumine our experience in dialogue with the church so that
it has purpose and direction. Will is the courage to act reflectively, not
in reaction, but with a vision of the Kingdom.

It is ultimately this vision to which we are called to be obedient,
which is why a concern for poverty and peace, traditionally the first
evangelical counsel, follows obedience in my ordering.

5. Poverty amid Plenty

RELIGION can provide a way to avoid the harsh facts of our experience, or it can be a means of living into the unpleasant actuality with reasonable hope. The spiritual life of the pastor or priest necessarily reflects his or her choice between those two alternatives. It is to be regretted that far too frequently the religion of escape characterizes the style of the ordained person, for indeed it is this that often receives the accolades of the powerful and wealthy.

Lewis Mumford in his discussion of Christianity in *The City in History*[1] makes the point that the church, as opposed to the pagan mystery religions of the ancient world, lived in the midst of the city. She faced the problems of the city and indeed included the city among the images of the new order. "So in the Spirit he carried me away to a great high mountain, and showed me the holy city of Jerusalem coming down out of heaven from God" (Rev. 21:10).

It is suggestive that our word "pagan" comes from the Latin *paganus*, which means "one who lives in a village," a "country yokel." It is important not to be simplistic, but a principal point of contact for Christian outreach in the first several centuries was among the urban poor, whose lives had become more and more meaningless. The satirists of the first century a.d. spoke of the populace who lived for "bread and circuses," the imperial dole and the chariot races and gladitorial combats used to appease the masses. They described the endless clamor of the city, punctuated with the frequent collapse of the *insulae*, the poorly constructed tenements for the poor. It was among the people of these tenements, living off the government dole, tranquilized by the ancient equivalent of television football, that the Gospel of Jesus Christ came with particular promise.

It is perhaps inaccurate to describe Jesus as one of the poor of his time. New Testament scholarship suggests that a carpenter would have been among the skilled artisans, roughly equivalent to the middle class of our day. But certainly our Lord was deeply concerned for the poor, and the early church understood him to have identified himself with the poor. Jesus is reported to have said, "Foxes have their holes, the birds their roosts; but the Son of Man has nowhere to lay his head" (Matt. 8:20). The preaching of the Gospel to the poor was considered an eschatological sign (Matt. 11:5), drawing on the imagery of Third Isaiah (Isaiah 61:1). Among the Beatitudes in Luke is the clear statement, "Blessed are the poor, because yours is the Kingdom of God" (Luke 6:20, translation mine). This is a much stronger version than found in Matthew, who softens it to speak of the "poor in spirit" (Matt. 5:3). Luke seems much closer to what we would expect of Jesus.

Certainly the identification with the poor has always been considered an instrumental value in Christian spiritual growth. Poverty is among the evangelical counsels. The saints of the past were often persons who embraced poverty and in many cases ministered to the poor. Francis of Assisi (1181/2–1226), the son of a wealthy merchant, gave everything away to beg his living so that he might be more like Christ. Catherine of Genoa (1447–1510), brought to indigence by her wastrel husband, turned their poverty into a virtue that they both might spend their lives ministering to the sick poor. Vincent de Paul (c.1580–1660), the co-founder of the Sisters of Charity, exercised a remarkable ministry in France to the ill and the indigent. Dorothy Day (1899–1980) of the Catholic Worker Movement lived among and cared for the poor of New York City.

It is interesting that when we think of those whose witness required that they identify with the poor, Roman Catholics come to mind most readily. While there were significant non-Roman Catholics concerned for the poor, there is no question but that Reformed theology's teaching concerning the fruits of election had its impact. The Protestant ethic implied that financial success was an indication of God's favor and this permeated post-Reformation, non-Roman Catholic thinking. Even Edward Bouverie Pusey (1800–1882), an early leader in the Catholic revival in Anglicanism, could preach in the poor houses of England no better a Gospel than one that patronized the poor and suggested that their suffering now might assure them a heaven later. He is also reported to have said that the debate in parliament over slavery was "piddling over a mere opinion."

Perhaps today the greatest insensitivity, ironically enough, to the plight of the poor is found among the leadership of the "electronic church," those who use today's media, primarily television, to prey upon the fears of the uneducated to solicit the "widow's mite." They are, of course, the direct descendents of American revivalism and its anticipation of the assurance of heaven in the experience of consolation. They preach for a decision evoked by an emotional crisis. All of this obscures issues of poverty and injustice that plague our cities and, consequently, is a sort of new paganism. Inasmuch as television isolates us from one another, the electronic preachers' principal medium reinforces a lack of social consciousness and blinds their viewers to the incongruence of their leaders' lifestyle—which often includes expensive houses, furnishings, clothes, cars, and yachts—with their own.

Certainly it is true that some congregations of poor and oppressed Christians act as if they want their pastor to appear affluent, driving about in an expensive car, dressed in silk suits, and enjoying the luxury of world travel. The affluent pastor becomes a symbol of the people's giving to God and a projection of their own fantasies. There is status in having an elegant preacher. The question is whether we play into this expectation or seek to create another.

As the power of classical Calvinism among the churches of the Reformation has waned and liberation theology, arising from South American Roman Catholicism, has spread among other denominations, we have seen in the last few decades a wider concern among Christians of various stripes for the poor. Modern understanding of social systems has grown, so in the spirit of Old Testament prophecy a compassion for the oppressed has now been added. Compare the Gospel, for example, of Mother Teresa of Calcutta with the message of the television preachers across our land. Dom Helder Camera, the Roman Catholic Bishop of Recife, who has no place to sleep but a cot in the sanctuary of his cathedral, has caught the imagination of thinking and praying Roman Catholics and non-Roman Catholics alike. The Sojourners, a group of evangelical Christians living in Washington, D.C., proclaim a Gospel that clearly identifies with the poor and the oppressed. Their lifestyle is in stark contrast to the image of affluence cultivated by the successful preachers of American righteousness.

It is doubtful that a strategy where all pastors sought to be like Dom Helder Camera or every Christian community like the Sojourners would be helpful. Identification with the poor is, as one person put it, "more an internal thing." Christian virtue calls for a universal consciousness of the meaning of poverty as it subverts the secular assumptions of Western civilization. The heroic witness of individual Christians like Mother Teresa becomes the road to our conscience and the symbol of the community that has at its best always embraced the plight of the urban poor and the oppressed.

Poverty as Symbol

In my interviews of clergy there was a general awareness of the issue of the church and the poor and oppressed, often joined by a sincere feeling of ambivalence about what this meant for their style of life. The following statement is an honest, characteristic reflection:

> I struggle with [the issue of poverty] a lot. I had some friends in my last church—we thought in terms of communal living. We thought of cutting way back in our lifestyle as far as the physical things. I don't know. Right now my feeling is a little more like—I wouldn't mind having a little more money to spend. I don't know whether that was just an age factor thing or what, but I'm not as strongly connected in my spirituality with my poverty. I think it gets very, very bad when things begin to provide the meaning for your life. At the same time I don't mind enjoying things. I'm probably a little less ascetic than I was five or six years ago.

The contrast between his nostalgia for a youthful enthusiasm and his present position tempered by inflation, family responsibilities, and a forgivable *joie de vivre* is rather poignant. The principle is clear: things must not provide the meaning for life. This man lived in a modest manse with a wife who worked and one child. With him I had no sense of someone who indulged himself, yet he struggled.

The struggle can be more intentional, that is, more purposeful and directed, if we understand poverty in the daily life of the ordained person as a symbol. We need to remind ourselves repeatedly that to classify something as a symbol does not make it less real, as our culture often thinks; rather we are designating it as a central image in our reality. Poverty as symbol becomes poverty as a way of seeing and living in the world.

Poverty does not mean penury. One does not have to become indigent, suffering from hunger and cold, to embrace poverty. Analogously, one does not have to become chemically dependent (i.e., an alcoholic, a drug addict) to know the horror of loneliness. The preponderance of evidence from the New Testament would suggest that our Lord and his disciples did not suffer from penury. It was noted that Judas Iscariot was the one who kept the common purse (John 13:29), so we can assume they had some means of support.

Penury is a problem to be overcome as poverty is a symbol to be embraced. Whether or not penury will ever be solved is another matter. The Fourth Evangelist is less sanguine—"For you have the poor among you always" (John 12:8)—than many modern social engineers. But we must be careful not to romanticize the poor, as Pusey appeared to do. There is no reason for thinking that poor folk are more holy than everyone else. Whatever Jesus may have meant in saying it is easier for a camel to pass through the eye of a needle than for a rich man to enter the Kingdom of Heaven, he was not recommending starvation as a means of acquiring the Kingdom of God. He was talking about poverty as a way of seeing and acting in the world (Matt. 19:24).

Poverty as a symbol has to do with receiving and giving. The priest or pastor is an instrumental image of the spiritual life, which life is an openness to God and a consequent openness to one another. The life in the spirit flows from a new transcendent awareness to an action grounded in the vision one shares with God. It is a continuous movement of receiving from God the gift of his presence and giving that gift to others. Poverty allows the freedom of that flow of God's presence through the life of the person, particularly the one who is ordained.

"Human fulfillment," says H. A. Williams, "cannot be reached along the road of gratified greed."[2] The investment of the self in things chokes the spirit, so that it is not capable of allowing the Spirit to slip into one's life. It is like going to an art gallery to view a painting. If one stands before a masterpiece with a mind filled with the countless interpretations from the past, there is little possibility that the painting may touch that person in a new and revealing manner. One must come empty to the painting; not empty in the sense of barren, but empty in the sense of being in an imaginal space full of possibilities.

A number of biblical images come to mind. The symbol of poverty is that of the well-tilled field, ready for the seed. I have in mind the parable-turned-into-allegory of the sower from the Gospel (Luke 8:4–15). The Gospel writer described four kinds of soil: that trodden underfoot, the rocky waste, the earth choked with weeds, and the good soil. Poverty-as-receiving pertains to the good soil, which is fertile with possibility.

We do not receive the word of God unless we are ready for it. A preoccupation with the acquisition of things obviously will drain our energy from that readiness. But curiously enough, so will a preoccupation with the need to pay for the necessities of life render us immune to God's solicitation. Herein is a twist that the modern money economy gives to the symbol of poverty. We do not live on a barter system: in an urban culture we cannot live off the land; and contemporary isolation destroys the spontaneous altruism of a community. If we are not to be "anxious about tomorrow" (Matt. 6:34)—that is, be free from that preoccupation—and trust in the Lord, it is necessary to have enough in the bank to pay the grocer. The specter of famine and cold in the lonely is not a "spiritual discipline."

Another biblical image of poverty-as-receiving is the contrast between purity of heart and serving both God and money (Matt. 5:8, 6:24). The person who is pure of heart possesses a simplicity of intention. The early church described the opposite of purity of heart as "two-souledness" or double-mindedness. The great value of this biblical image is its relation to consciousness and individual and corporate intention. The heart is the biblical image for those emotions, intuitions, and thoughts that make up our consciousness. Purity of heart calls for an undiverted, fixed focus of awareness on our God-given goal in life. The double-minded person has a fuzzy, unfocused intentionality.

In the research for this study it appeared often that the persons interviewed had a hunch about what it means to be pure in heart, but there was not much clarity. They were a remarkably centered group of people, but not very articulate about their own inner meaning. It was as if the world were conspiring to keep them diverted from a clear flow of grace through themselves as instruments of the divine. Poverty is a symbol of what we need.

Poverty is also giving. One cannot give what one has not received. One priest told me of a woman in his parish who said to him bluntly, "It appears to me that you are trying to give us what you do not have." The hurt is justified if it actually reflects the situation, or as in this case, it changes how we live. Efforts to go contrary to the principle that we must receive in order to give result in quick clergy burnout. But if we have received the word of God, then we must not sit on it like the man who buried his talent or bag of gold (Matt. 25:14–30).

A priest of some fifteen years was describing to me the history of his homiletical style. Early in his ministry he had delivered carefully prepared essays on topical issues of the day, assuring himself that everything he said could be documented by reliable sources. Something had happened to him along the way and now he found himself, as he put it, standing in the pulpit "playing God." He was preaching what he believed and he was scared! But, he went on to explain, the people were acting as if they were being fed. As I listened it seemed to me that this priest, who at the same time explained to me that he did not know what "spirituality" meant, had stumbled onto the gift of poverty. He was not playing God; in that pulpit he was God, giving himself through him to the people. That is something worth our fear. "It is a terrible thing to fall into the hands of the living God" (Heb. 10:31).

Christianity believes in a God who "emptied himself, taking the form of a servant" (Phil. 2:7, rsv). This is not emptying oneself so as to exhaust one's energy and resources. This is to empty oneself as the springs and lakes in Minnesota empty themselves to form the Mississippi River. There is an infinite grace or presence that flows unimpeded from God through Christ into his creation for the sake of life. What is characteristic of God needs to be characteristic of God's people. Poverty is a symbol that enables our emptying.

Needs and Resources

The symbol of poverty is a provocative complement to an increasing awareness that population growth and the lack of additional arable land threaten to face us with a worldwide catastrophe in another generation, according to *The Global 2000 Report to the President*.[3] It becomes an issue of the discernment of needs and sharing. It is not now a matter of available fossil fuels, which appear sufficient for the next few centuries, but of the unequal distribution of those fuels, their cost, and the lack of an adequate and/or sufficient substitute. Increased productivity of the land is dependent upon these fossil fuels.

This is not to preach doomsday, which is sometimes the barbed caricature of those who prefer in regard to the issues of the future an ostrichlike stance characteristic of contemporary Western culture. It is to raise a question as to whether the acquisition of "more" for its own sake is not a lifestyle fated to bring disaster not too far down the line.

An ever increasing number of people wanting more, when more is not a possibility on this planet, can only result in violence of an unimaginable kind. There is a prophetic judgment placed upon us and this demands a new consciousness, a spirit of poverty.

One of the persons interviewed for this book, a man who has spent part of his ministry working on matters related to world hunger, observed:

> In many ways we [the clergy] have bought into the success culture. We need to be successful and that finds its fulfillment in material ways. So therefore on one level clergy see themselves on a par with other professions and have allowed the other professions to set the standards.

The fact that we have allowed these standards to become the criteria of success in the ordained ministry, this person continued to say, is a result of our search for an identity as priests or pastors in terms of the accepted social norms. There is a loss, he implied, of a sense of a transcendent vocation, which has a very different set of standards of success. It is on this, among other things, that the projections of a growing scarcity of resources places a judgment.

Among some of the early church fathers it was thought that death was not simply a curse, but also a blessing in disguise. For with death came the demise of the physical body and with its passage the temptation to sin left us. There is no doubt that this identification of temptation with the body, while quite Pauline (Gal. 5:16–17), is inadequate. But it is possible that we can use the same argument to say that the limitation of resources in this world may free us to discover the richness of a life not given over to the gratification of greed.

What should happen is that our use of the created world becomes related to need, our own and our neighbor's need. I am not suggesting a loss of a certain *joie de vivre* of the kind the pastor I quoted earlier enjoyed. To the contrary, in the freedom that comes from no longer needing to acquire possessions as a measure of our worth we may find a greater pleasure in the material world of things. H. A. Williams comments, "Poverty is the ability to enjoy the world to the full because I am not anxious about losing a bit of it or acquiring a bit of it." He goes on to say, "Poverty also consists of the recognition that I have within my own resources ample enough . . . to meet [life] creatively, so that it builds me up into my own selfhood."[4]

I come from a family of fast eaters. My father, who was occasionally absent-minded and might fall on his food as soon as his plate arrived in front of him, was capable of finishing his meal before my mother was served. I have found my own habit of wolfing my food a social handicap. It therefore struck me with particular meaning when I read Tilden Edwards' description in *Living Simply Through the Day* [5] how one might eat attentively and become the master of his appetite. The idea is to enjoy eating more by meditating upon the food itself. There is a sensuality to this approach that, far from promoting either disdain for the material world or greed, in fact relates food to our needs in a way that encourages sheer enjoyment.

Among the interviews were two comments that come to mind at this point. One delightful Irish priest in speaking of the relationship of needs to resources reported to me a comment he made to a pastor, whose new rectory he had just toured: "I couldn't live here because I couldn't go to the front door with no shoes and socks on." The house was in control of the person and pure pleasure in one's surroundings was not a possibility. Another pastor, more polished perhaps than the former, spoke of a need to avoid extremes, but then complained sadly of the younger clergy who were given to running around in designer jeans and knit shirts with embroidered alligators. The "preppy pastor" was too much for him.

What these two pastors were saying is that there was a disjuncture between needs and resources. We do not need opulent rectories; we do not need to wear designer jeans and shirts. Is it an appropriate use of resources that inhibits that detachment from things the ordained person might cultivate? One could debate the particulars of these illustrations, but it is true that an attachment to rich living chokes that quiet, inner space in which one is able to hear the Spirit. We become "double-souled."

Yet this takes a more immediate focus in the light of the growing inequity between the needs of the world as a whole and our consumption. It may just be that we need to eat more chicken and fish and less beef and cook it efficiently. Certainly water is rapidly becoming a more precious commodity and we as a habit waste it. As my wife reminds me, I need to stop shaving with the water running. One of those interviewed suggested that he did not think it right that he drive a Cadillac; but this is not just so he will not appear ostentatious. There is a question of fuel economy. We also might live down the wide reputation of clergy as reckless and fast drivers. Should the clergy residence be heated to more than 65 degrees or cooled to less than 78 degrees? These are issues that are not just practical expedients—national programs by which we demonstrate our patriotism—but symptoms of our own intentionality.

One indication of those who are truly evangelized is the ability to discern the signs of the times. Moralism is the enemy of the spiritual life. But morality is the fruit of that life, and if we have heard the Gospel it will show itself by our sensitivity to the particular ways in which God calls us to behave in this age. I do not think there is any question about that and certainly the ordained are called to lead in this new awareness.

Mortification

In the medieval world any lord of the manor who could afford one had a court jester. The task of the jester was to remind the lord of his own humanity through the medium of ribald humor, lest in his illusions of power he think too well of himself. When I first started speaking at clergy conferences in 1970 I discovered that many clergy groups had their own clowns, whose task was not to remind us of our humanity, but to seduce us into thinking we did not have to worry about it.

On one occasion that I vividly recall the leader had us process about the grounds of a local school, carrying helium-filled balloons inscribed with the words, "Up with Jesus." Other than the fact that it was unpleasantly cold outside that day, I remember that we were marched into the chapel—much to the relief of my frozen feet—and at the reading of the Gospel were instructed to release the balloons, which were last seen bouncing against the vaulting of the ceiling. I would like to say the reading was from Luke's account of Jesus' ascension, but I cannot recall that for sure!

These clerical clowns were given to wearing buttons saying "Celebrate Life," which was bad enough, but they insisted that others wear them as well. I know a pastor who is still wearing his ten years later. I thought of this as I read these words from Edward Hays, a Roman Catholic spiritual guide:

> Among the numerous duties of a disciple, two are essential: to embrace a discipline in life not only in theory, but also in daily practice, and to fall in love with death![6]

I purposely used the old-fashioned word "mortification" to head up this section because it implies a falling in love with death and has certain shock value.

Any good gardener knows that beautiful roses require careful pruning. Pieces of living plant have to die. It cannot just grow wild. We cannot simply "celebrate growth." It is more than to be regretted, it is tragic that we seem to have lost the insight that growth in Christ requires careful pruning. Pieces of us by our intentional action need to die if we are to become the person that is in God's vision. We are not cutting away a cancerous growth, but making room for intended growth. Mortification refers to that intentional action of pruning life that better life might grow by God's grace—just as better roses grow by God's grace. Undoubtedly there have been people who have thought that by mortifying themselves they earned merit with God. But as T. S. Eliot put in the mouth of Thomas à Becket:

> The last temptation is the greatest treason
> To do the right deed for the wrong reason.[7]

There is always this temptation. For Becket it was to die that he might be remembered as a great martyr. In Eliot's play Becket found the right reason for being martyred. Similarly, finding the wrong reasons for mortification does not mean there are no right reasons. One right reason for mortification is to remind us of our humanity—what is and what might be—as the court jesters did for the kings of old.

Mortification is the intentional denial of legitimate pleasures in the spirit of Christian poverty that one might become more human. In my tradition Lent has long been considered a time for mortification, although one would not use such a "medieval" word. We gave up eating, desserts, going to movies, or telling dirty jokes, all of which in the face of world problems seemed rather trivial. Once rendered silly, we dismissed the idea of "giving up" and talked of "taking on." What we failed to understand was that a life incapable of significant sacrifice is also incapable of courageous action.

On a couple of occasions in the early 1970s I shared the podium with the anthropologist Margaret Mead. It is perhaps unknown by the majority of her followers, but Mead was a devout church person. She had little patience with the ecclesiastical version of the "flower children," for whom life was always a celebration. Standing with her walking stick in hand (I never saw her without it), she would pronounce with a wave of her stick, "No fast, no feast."

She was right. A fundamental principle of the spiritual life is its os-cillation between mortification and celebration. The church year teaches it and this only reflects life. Calvary was no accident on the way to the Empty Tomb; it was a necessary precondition. The New Testa-ment is very explicit in suggesting that the disciple *intentionally* take up his or her cross and follow Jesus, which is more than merely accepting the one someone else lays on you. Which is to say that the removal of the Friday fast in Roman Catholicism, which was aped by many An-glicans, does not lift from the disciple the responsibility to fast. The Friday fast may have become trivialized and may have needed to be abandoned, but the responsibility for significant fasting did not evapo-rate—it now rests with us.

On one occasion during a children's homily at which I was pres-ent, the priest asked the children if they knew what fasting was. One child piped up, "Starving for twenty-four hours." There is an appro-priate identification with the hungry in that definition, for they are perpetually threatened with starvation. One commentator on the issue of mortification, particularly in relation to needs and resources, said, "The whole issue of food became my key into [the simpler life]."

Generally fasting, the act of eating nothing, and abstinence, the act of refraining from certain foods or drink, are the common forms of mortification in contemporary Christian practice. Perhaps one might add protracted periods of silence as a fasting from talk. Abbreviated sleep, flagellation, and perhaps even hair shirts have not altogether vanished. But even in an age as given to Encratism as the fourteenth century, Henry Suso (c.1295–1366) ended up tossing his portable self-torture apparatus into the Rhine. He became aware of its self-cen-teredness. Excessive mortification easily slips into its dark side: pride in outdoing one another or ourselves at it.

In the sample of clergy interviewed, on the mean they indicated that they found self-denial from food, drink, and coitus occasionally helpful in their spiritual journey (3.07 on a scale of 1 to 5, n = 14). No one spoke of it as never helpful, and there was no significant de-nominational distinction. This is not surprising, but it was somewhat unexpected that the body on the mean was seen occasionally as an impediment to spiritual growth (2.71 on a scale of 1 to 5, n = 14). I am reminded of Augustine of Hippo's (354–430) lament that whereas he would have ascended to God, he was weighed down by his body. The imagery of Neo-Platonism is not totally alien to our sample.

The attitude toward self-denial corresponds to a slight preference for an apophatic (i.e., emptying) style of prayer among those interviewed, (nine out of twelve) as compared to a kataphatic (i.e., imaging) style. Apophatic prayer is in the Dionysian or Byzantine tradition, which was profoundly influenced by the desert fathers and their search for purity of heart. The spirit of poverty in this instance is to live as retaining nothing, but letting all things pass through our minds and hearts.

One testimony in the interviews to the power of fasting speaks for many who have found this a valuable spiritual discipline in the spirit of apophatic prayer.

> The whole cycle of fasting brought something that I cannot really explain. Not having food over a period of time also seemed to do something, not only psychologically, but mentally . . . When I did my prayer or Bible study or even in conversations, after twenty-four hours or so, there was another whole awareness. There was something about it that was calling other things into play that the food seemed to have repressed . . . If the lifestyle is to give you a whole new perception on life, then I can say that just that aspect [of fasting] helped me see things in different ways . . . It was something new for me.

This priest wanted to make clear that he was speaking only for himself, but his witness is in accord with instrumental images to assist us in a new awareness of God in the world.

There is another form of self-denial that is important for a new awareness of God. I was struck by one person's comment that for him prayer is "a means of attentiveness as opposed to a means of salvation, that is, a way to get something." It is so easy for every act of ministry to be justified in our minds on the basis of what we get from it—money, merit, friends, popularity, success, or salvation. A very difficult form of fasting is to act with no intention of any kind of reward, but just as an expression of faithful service. Can we justify the question: What is in it for me?

This sacrifice of the ego may well indeed lead us deeper into the self, which the ego has for so long defended. For mortification does not kill the self, it creates room for it to grow.

Peacemaking

Poverty is related not only to purity of heart, but to the other parables, including that of peacemaking. "How blest are the peacemakers; God shall call them his sons" (Matt. 5:9). The word "peace" means health and wholeness, not just the opposite of war. It is a characteristic of the Kingdom of God and so it is the product of the new awareness to which Jesus calls us in preaching repentance and which is the key to our spiritual life. A test of our shared vision with God is our ability to act as instruments of God's peace.

Thomas Merton wrote as clearly on this subject as anyone. He made it clear that the issue for the Christian is not pacifism. It is a question of how the church might meet most effectively the evil in the world, which stands in the way of the Christian goal: God's reign over his creation. Our strategy is to *resist* evil. This may require force on occasion, although Merton argued that the most effective tactic in the resistance of evil is nonviolence. But first we must be clear about the objective, which is peace, the health and wholeness of society. Then—and only then—we have to affirm what logically follows: that we resist evil. The issue for every Christian finally, after the first two steps, becomes how evil is best resisted. If with Merton we conclude that the best tactic is nonviolence, we must never confuse nonviolence with nonresistance.

Furthermore, in suggesting the possibility of a tactic of nonviolence, it does *not* follow that Christian spirituality is naive. Often the world will judge nonviolence to be ingenuous—perhaps because it requires the remarkable courage and self-knowledge most of us lack—despite the rather impressive evidence to the contrary (e.g., Mahatma Gandhi and Martin Luther King, Jr.). The caricature of the peacemaker as a milksop is more a dismissal of the judgment in his or her witness rather than an accurate description of the personality. Our Lord sent out the Twelve to preach with the admonition that they "become as shrewd as serpents, unmixed with evil as doves" (Matt. 10:16, translation mine). Political acumen and a profound knowledge of human perversity are part of spiritual maturity. As one priest put it, quoting John of the Cross, a spiritual director must be absolutely unshockable.

Evidently the distinction between the objective, strategy, and tactics of action born of Christian prayer has become confused in the minds of many clergy. At least, this is the implication of some of the interviews, particularly as relates to peace. When the subject of peace-making arose, one response was the explanation that the pastor or priest is not a pacifist, as if that were synonymous with peacemaking. This confusion also reflects itself in another person who suggested that peace means reconciliation, but then added that he needed to think about it more. As he proceeded to think, he related reconciliation to tolerance.

The root of the New Testament word for reconciliation, *allassō*, means to "change" or "alter" something. *Katallāgē*, the word for "reconciliation"—as in God "has enlisted us in this service of reconciliation" (2 Cor. 5: 18)—means a *fundamental change*. It is quite the opposite of tolerance. When we perform this ministry we can be assured of evoking conflict. Evil is not going to surrender without a fight. The question is not whether we should seek peace and overcome evil, but how we best do this. Clarity of thought among the clergy would sharpen this issue. One priest did speak to this point when he said, "I think peace is one of those priceless words of the Christian tradition that is never exhausted in terms of bringing together those things that appear to be opposite."

I doubt that there is a much more commonly misunderstood Christian principle than the nature of reconciliation. Again and again the leadership of the church invokes reconciliation as a strategy when they mean the suppression of conflict and the appearance of harmony. In many ways reconciliation is more a synonym for repentance, which can only lead to the conflict supremely expressed in the cross. The church can make no peace with oppression.

Perhaps a test of the lucidity of mind that comes from prayer is whether or not we can discern the difference between good and evil. When there is a hesitancy for us to go on the offensive in the fight on behalf of peace it may be because we are not sure in ourselves of the difference. It is difficult to determine whether this reticence is a result of a lack of moral vision or an avoidance of the inevitable conflict that comes with standing by one's convictions. I am unwilling to say that the research sample on the whole lacked a toughness that could endure conflict—they seemed to be quite capable of taking care of themselves in a fight—but I was left with the feeling that the implications of peacemaking had not been well thought out by most of them for one reason or another.

I recall many years ago a friend of mine visiting me at the seminary at which I then served. He was a man who prided himself on knowing the difference between right and wrong, but in a moralistic, black-and-white manner. Before I realized it the seminary had come under his attack because, unlike him, he was saying, we no longer held to moral principles. I suspect we were as much to blame for his erroneous impression as he was for making this judgment. This is because in resisting the simplistic definitions of good and evil and the tactics they evoke, we had failed to make common cause with him in the service of the Christian objective of the Kingdom of God and the strategy of resistance to evil.

Our prayer could profit from a reflection upon the distinctions between objectives, strategies, and tactics in order that we might make our witness known in the service of the divine vision.

Conclusion

It is clear that there is no widespread feeling among ordained persons in our parishes that the Gospel requires of us today a heroic pursuit of material poverty. The witness of a few persons, particularly in the Third World, is admired but not emulated. It would be inaccurate to say that this is the result of an indifference toward the sufferings of other people. There is ample evidence that world hunger, the agony of war, and the oppression of minorities is a cause for concern among us.

There is a compassion among the clergy that finds immediate expression. One woman in this sample is known for giving the clothes off her back—almost literally—to those with less. She told me of her sister taking her shopping for clothes on one occasion only after the sister had elicited the promise that she would keep these clothes and not give them away.

But as is often the case our acts of compassion are more or less *ad hoc.* They are not expressions of a consistent understanding of poverty, purity of heart, and peacemaking as characteristic of the Christian posture within the world. There is a lack of that analytical clarity that gives integrity to the Gospel witness and shapes the cutting edge of our fight against the evils of greed and covetousness.

6. Sexuality and Holiness

A PRIEST told me of a dream he had that he found both fascinating and alarming. But first there is the background to the dream. The priest was in the midst of considerable controversy in his parish. His ministry had been called into question on a broad front and he was in much emotional pain. From two nuns on the staff of his parish he had received considerable support during this time. The dream was very brief, but memorable. He saw our Lord hanging upon the cross. One of the nuns stood on either side of Jesus and in order to comfort him they were stroking him in an obviously sexual manner.

My hunch is that in this dream the priest saw his suffering as an identification with the Passion of our Lord. His conflict in the parish was an occasion both of great suffering and of the opportunity for spiritual growth. But what made a source of pain an occasion of grace was the acceptance he found in the two women, whose femininity was identified both with his genital yearning and the more generalized longing for oneness and acceptance that is focused in our sexual desire.

There is no doubt that some experiencing this dream would be uncomfortable, if not scandalized. There is the common assumption, born of centuries of Christian teaching and practice, that spirituality and sexuality are antithetical. As one person interviewed explained, "There is no one way you can see God, there is no way you can possess him even here, if one is not a chaste—striving to be a chaste and repentantly a chaste person." Of course, this does not define the word "chaste," which can mean many things from not being guilty of illicit sexual intercourse to being modest to being celibate. This brings us to the third evangelical counsel: chastity.

One of the better kept secrets in the spiritual life is that, far from being opposites, sexuality and spirituality are very closely related. This can be understood only by defining carefully the word "sexuality." One priest spoke of himself in these words, "People say, 'You're not married. What do you do about sex?' I say, 'I say Mass.'" Earlier he observed, "Sexuality is the expression of the whole personality, as I understand it; so is my spiritual life." Obviously, he means something different by sexuality than many people understand, yet not entirely different.

Sexuality encompasses a person's mind, spirit, and emotions, as well as his or her body. It is impossible for us to meet someone else except as a sexual person, just as we cannot meet another except as a spiritual person. Sexuality names the *desire* each person has to have a relationship with others and it defines the *mode* of that relationship. In other words, sexuality denotes both a movement and a process in the interaction between individuals. It also connotes a self-awareness that comes into consciousness in that interaction, as well as reflects the manner in which we perceive ourselves in that relationship.

The correspondence to our definition of spirituality should be evident. *Sexuality* presumes an openness on the part of one subject to relationship with another subject at some level of intimacy that involves the total person—mind, spirit, emotions, and body—although it does not necessarily involve a genital relationship. In that act of intimacy it is possible that a new consciousness of the self in the world may develop, which will be in terms of our own history and will be evident in our actions. This covers four of the five points in the definition of spirituality. A complete congruence between sexuality and spirituality depends upon the intention of sexuality for transcendence, which I believe is the final cause of human sexuality.

Previous generations were just as much sexual persons as we are, but because of their history they were perhaps less explicitly aware of the relationship of the body and emotions to the mind and spirit and were more willing to affirm the cultural stereotypes of men and women and their interaction than are we. In the last generation or so Western culture has become more differentiated in its sexual awareness. This is our contemporary history, which is our burden and our opportunity. In our awareness we have discovered that there is an inescapable relationship between personality and physiology that is deeper than those sexual roles imposed by society and is evocative of modes of consciousness that pertain to both men and women and are called "masculine" and "feminine."

Unlike the people of previous centuries, therefore, we can no longer pretend to strive for some form of spiritual asexuality. A castrated man is simply a gelded male. A woman past menopause is simply a woman beyond the climacteric. We can complain about the burden of our bodies, but there is no unisex and we are all sexual. D. H. Lawrence was right, our understanding and use of that sexuality shapes our world and there is no other world. We must live in this world and strive to become whole.

So whatever chastity may mean, it cannot mean living a life of repression or in some charade of sexlessness. The sexuality rooted in our bodies will come "out" in relationships, our language, and our contemplation of the divine mystery. What chastity *does* mean, according to H. A. Williams, is "the capacity so to sift my experience as to be enlarged and enriched by it instead of being diminished or destroyed."[1]

The Misuse of History

There are various ways that Christians support their present attitudes about sexuality by referring to the church's past. They are usually wrong.

The most common is supposedly to contrast a Hebrew positive evaluation of sex and marriage to be found in the Bible and a Greek negative attitude toward sex, which captured the church in the second or third generation of its existence. Such a distinction is a caricature of the facts. There was a difference between Hebrew attitudes in the tenth century b.c. and Greek in the fourth century b.c., but not what we generally think. More accurately, Hebrew men considered women as property to be enjoyed, Greek men considered women property too dangerous to be enjoyed. Both cultures were strongly patriarchal, but not without occasional insights into the symbolic meaning of sexuality and its spiritual implications. The story of Hosea and Gomer, for example, is a moving metaphor of God's love for humanity. But we have to be peculiarly insensitive to fail to see the depth of love between husband and wife in the Greek tragedies of the fifth century b.c. as an expression of divine goodness in human form as well.

By the time Jewish and Hellenistic thought are in close interaction, it is difficult to make neat distinctions between the two. Greek philosophy may have encouraged dualism, although even that is debatable. The Platonism of the Intertestamental and New Testament times is strongly influenced by Stoicism, which is a kind of monism. Certainly popular Hellenistic culture admired the human body. It was this admiration of the nude form that, among other things, offended the Jews at the time of Antiochus Epiphanes (d. 163 b.c.) and led to the Maccabean rebellion. It was rabbinical puritanism that lay behind the words attributed to Jesus by Matthew concerning adultery (Matt. 5:28), and indeed it was the rabbis who first taught that cleanliness is next to godliness. This certainly encourages a practical, if not philosophical, dualism.

The ancient Jewish expectation that women should marry and bear children had no higher motivation than does the chauvinism of the American South reflected in the admonition to keep one's wife "barefoot and pregnant." If we take Paul at face value, his words seem to imply a functional dualism, where celibacy is to be preferred to marriage (1 Cor. 7:9). Certainly the Pauline letters supported for centuries the widely accepted Christian spiritual virtue of *apatheia*, freedom from irrational passion. There is no reason to look beyond the Jewish tradition to explain the reference in Revelation to the 144,000 on Mount Zion who were ransomed, "who did not defile themselves with women" (Rev. 14:4).

A somewhat less common misuse of history is to accuse Christians over the first nineteen hundred years of being perverse. Without doubt the almost universal theological assumption that human sexuality existed solely for the procreation of children was not seriously challenged over that period of time. But this opinion followed logically from a major premise, to wit: to be human is to be a rational mind, which has no substantial relationship to the human body. The minor premise was that the destroyer of the rational mind is irrational (as distinct from rational) passion. Since the most obvious experience of irrational passion is coitus, celibacy was the choice of the chaste. They knew that sexual intercourse was necessary, just as someone has to sow wheat to get more wheat, but the aim was to reduce the passion in its performance. This is why church fathers said it was wrong to lust after one's wife.

There is no doubt that sexual intercourse is an experience of irrational passion. Thinking can interfere with performance. The problem with past Christian understanding of sexuality is the major premise that to be human is to be pure rationally, which was held by most thinking people—Christian and non-Christian—for at least two thousand years. When Augustine of Hippo was converted to Christianity, he cruelly dismissed his mistress—much to the delight of his nasty mother. The implication was that now Augustine had to practice what he believed—actually believed *before* he was converted. In my judgment the dismissal of his mistress was a greater sin against chastity than his years of occupying her bed. But this is because I do not believe what he believed about true humanity. Augustine did what was for his times the logical thing. But in sifting his experience so that he might enlarge and enrich his life, he ignored the fact that his mistress had forever enriched his life by giving him her body. But this is twentieth-century thinking. It does no good to berate Augustine for not understanding as a twentieth-century instead of a fifth-century man.

A third misuse of history arises from the second. If it is a mistake to attack conclusions from the past, without recognizing the hypothesis from which they were drawn, it is an even greater mistake to impose those norms in our society without examining their premises in the light of contemporary knowledge. When in the fall of 1980 Pope John Paul II said, for example, that a husband must not lust after his wife, he was, as already noted, reaffirming an ancient Christian admonition. It struck most contemporary people, however, as ridiculous because we do not believe that passion is the destroyer of humanity. Of course, it was explained that he meant men should not make sexual objects of their wives, which is in accordance with contemporary knowledge, but he chose the language drawn from an entirely different set of premises.

It is interesting to note in this light what has happened to the notion of celibacy. In the interviews no one argued that being in the state of marriage disqualifies one from becoming a priest on the grounds that life without sexual intercourse is a "higher way" and those who are ordained are called to a higher form of spirituality. One Roman Catholic priest spoke very directly about his belief that some priests should be married. No married pastors railed against celibacy, even if they spoke warmly of their own marriage. It was seen as an option for some. The argument in favor of celibacy was either one of expedience—it leaves one freer to exercise ministry—or symbolism—it stands for the marriage between Christ and his church.

Historically marriage has been the institution by which the chastity of sexual intercourse is assured. When those interviewed were asked to agree or disagree with the statement, "It is possible for sexual intercourse outside of marriage to be a source of spiritual illumination," two disagreed and five strongly disagreed, as we might expect. But five stated they were undecided about this and two agreed. Re-

member, though, that we are not dealing with a sample skewed unre-
alistically toward youth or liberal theological views. The median age of
this sample is forty-four and the average age is forty-six. Theologically
the group tended to fall in a center to right-of-center position. The response becomes more interesting in the case of the statement, "A solid
marriage leads to a deeper experience of God than a life of solitude."
Three strongly agreed, including one Roman Catholic priest, two
agreed, three were undecided, and six disagreed! This did not break
down along the lines of the celibate and the married. An educated
guess of what this means is that the unequivocal relationship between
constructive mating and marriage is eroding, as well as the Reformation mystique of the solid marriage as the ground of spiritual maturity.
Human sexuality as expressed in sexual intercourse is seen in a
broader, more ambiguous context than marriage.

Obviously we have moved away from the past premises of Christian teaching on sexuality. An understanding of the human being as
essentially one in mind, spirit, emotions, and body is ever more firmly
established in the church's teaching. The fact that those interviewed
almost exclusively preferred a speculative (i.e., of the head) style of
prayer to an affective (i.e., of the heart) would suggest that the mind is
seen as dominant. Sexuality is very much a part of this, however, and
if spirituality is a capacity of the whole person we would expect the life
of prayer to involve both a sexual imagery in its expression and an enrichment of our sexuality in all its dimensions.

A Contemporary Theological Premise

I have discussed the human being as an integral union of those aspects
we often think of separately—mind, spirit, emotions, body. The mind's
capacity for self-awareness lifts this coalescence of body and emotion
to that level of being that the Bible describes as the image of God. The
mind is the soil in which God plants the seed of his Word and from
which springs the will. But behind this understanding of humans lies
a more fundamental presumption about God's creation. It is that life
is *dynamic, dialectic,* and *teleological.*

Life is *dynamic* as opposed to static. One thing that is certain is
that we all change: individuals, cultures, institutions, and the cosmos
itself. In fact, it is the movement that keeps creation from imploding,
falling in on itself. What is static is dead. We are sustained by energy,

from the particles that rotate about the nucleus of the atom to the ever expanding universe. To be is to be moved by an uncreated energy that is from God. In fact, we know God by his energy, not by any direct knowledge of what he is (i.e., his essence).

Life is *dialectic* as opposed to linear. Truth is bimodal. It emerges in the tension between two contrary, but not mutually destructive, poles. This can be imagined in a number of ways, but the one I find most helpful is that of a journey that requires an oscillation through two states of consciousness or two ways of constructing our world: the analytical and the metaphorical modes. We are always moving away from one and toward the other, just as one must either climb the Mountain of the Transfiguration with Jesus or come down from it (Luke 9:28–45). One cannot stay there. Jesus himself journeyed from the wilderness to the city and back again, over and over.

Life is *teleological* as opposed to entelechial. This is to say that what happens is not caused only by what is past, but also by what is in the future. There is a purpose to creation. Life is goal oriented. The life, death, and resurrection of Jesus speak to us about the future more than the past. History is going somewhere of which the Incarnation is a prolepsis.

Inasmuch as life is dynamic, dialectic, and teleological, human sexuality is the symbol of this reality. Symbols correspond to what they represent, that is, they possess an analogous relationship to that to which they point. For example, the wine in the Eucharist has a bouquet, a vibrancy, and a character that leads us to speak of the "life" in the wine, which is analogous to the life in Christ's blood. Sexuality involves the total human being—mind, spirit, emotions, and body—in a dynamic, dialectic, and teleological relationship that is analogous to all of life.

Human sexuality is *dynamic* because it is the expression of eros, the energy innate in a human being for oneness with another. At one level eros is that gnawing desire to possess the other, beginning with a horny, delicious, physical pain. It is an emotion that gives rise to such synonyms for sexual intercourse as "to have" someone. This is not the genital expression of human sexuality at its most sublime and lies at the root of the church's distrust of the body and its suspicion of lust. Yet it is the flip side of a longing to be possessed or caught up in a greater presence.

Eros is that energy that has immense capacity to evoke action and reaction. Wars have been fought in the name of eros, murders are committed every day for its sake, and the commerce of great countries dances to its tune. All this is perhaps obvious. But it is equally important to remember that eros, cleansed of its irrational passion, has from the first centuries of Christian spirituality been understood as the heart's natural longing for God. Corrupted, impotent, it nonetheless is what drives folk upward toward God in an effort for union with the one, which would be futile if it were not for God meeting us in the *agapē*, of his son's Passion and lifting us up to his presence.

Much of this understanding shows itself in the fondness of the spiritual masters of the past for the Song of Songs or the Canticle. This lovely, explicit love poem, filled with delightful double entendres, has provided the imagery for Origen, Gregory of Nyssa, Bernard of Clairvaux, John of the Cross, and countless others to tell us of the nature of humanity's quest for God, and God's unfailing courtship of us. The author of Song of Songs writes (2:8):

> Hark! My beloved! Here he comes,
> bounding over the mountains, leaping over the hills.
> My beloved is like a gazelle.

What neither the English text nor the Greek or Latin used by our forefathers tells us is that in Hebrew to leap like a gazelle also means to "hump" as in to copulate. Even in the minds of those for whom sexual intercourse was a less than human activity there is a common root in the erotic energy that gives life both to our physical desires and our spiritual longings.

In the priest's dream mentioned at the beginning of the chapter there is an identification of sacrificial suffering with erotic longing. To sacrifice is to "make holy" or whole or one. The common dynamic of genitality and sanctification is infused with the common energy of eros.

Human sexuality is *dialectic* at its very base. No one would dispute the fact that coitus requires a minimum of two persons for a satisfying experience. This suggests some dialectic arrangement. From this point on, however, there is continuing debate. Without being drawn into an extensive argument, I would contend that the physical fact of sexual intercourse is a sacramental expression of the union of two total persons—mind, spirit, and emotions, as well as body—requiring for a meeting in depth that it be limited to two persons. Whereas I am willing to acknowledge that a genital homosexual relationship can be a genuine expression of love, I would maintain that there is a symbolic incongruity in homosexual intercourse. We are embodied creatures, and the nature of our bodies is not a matter of indifference to the most profound of life's meaning: symbolic reality.

Masculinity and femininity as terms used to denote modes of consciousness lie at the root of creation and human existence. Both modes of consciousness are present in each person, male or female. Whereas undoubtedly much of what we identify as characteristic of men and women are cultural stereotypes, this is not true of the most fundamental meanings of those words. Whether buried in the genes, a racial memory, or emanating from the mystery of being (any and all of which I consider a possibility), masculinity and femininity reflect a dialectic in life that is essential to human existence. When one or the other is allowed to dominate or repress the other, culture suffers and may die. Humanity requires a vital culture for its existence and growth.

So basic is the sexual dialectic in life that when the Priestly writers in Genesis spoke of humans being made in the image of God, they followed this with a reference to the creation of humankind as male and female. We seem to sense a congruity between the sexuality of people and the source of all creation. Throughout the history of religion there has been the need to describe God in terms of either masculinity or femininity. Whichever way God is pictured, it shapes our particular conception of transcendence as it is known in the world. As we first uncover the religious notions of *Homo sapiens*, the divine is dominated by a feminine deity, generically called the great mother. Around 2000 b.c., give or take a thousand years, there was a dramatic shift in much religious thinking to a masculine supreme deity, such as the Hebrew Yahweh.

What is more fitting is to understand God as neither one sex nor the other—not asexual, but androgynous. During the last four thousand years under a masculine deity the feminine continues underground to erupt occasionally to enrich our belief. The cult of the Blessed Virgin is only one more appealing example of this.

When Thomas Merton fell in love with his nurse in the hospital, to which he came for a hemorrhoidectomy, his thoughts turned to Eve, Mary, "Jesus our Mother," and *Hagia Sophia* ("Holy Wisdom"), the Christian symbols of the feminine in God. Sophia is God who comes to us, as Merton says, from

> the depths of the divine fecundity . . . She is the candor of God's light, the expression of His simplicity . . . Sophia is the

unknown, the dark, the nameless Ousia [primal being] . . .
the inexhaustible source of the creative realizations, of the
Father's glory . . . Sophia is the mercy of God in us . . .
[Sophia embodies] the one thing greater than glory [which]
is weakness, nothingness, poverty.[2]

If we were to think of these words as only the moonings of a love-
sick, middle-aged monk, we would miss the point. They may be that
as well, but they are also the considered thoughts of a spiritual theologian who saw in the poignancy of his own love a reflection of the nature of the cosmos and the God who created it. The dialectic of sexual
love mirrors the creative love that abides ultimately in God.

In the dream of our Lord on the cross, the spiritual spouse of the
two women who caressed him, the priest experienced the restorative
power of the feminine. He was locked in battle between his own masculine and the congregation contaminated by its collective, destructive
feminine. But the two nurturing women healed his perspective and
gave balance to his life in that congregation by recalling him to his own
creative feminine. An unhealthy dialectic was countered by a healthy
one. The phallus of the cross was accepted into the womb/tomb of the
earth, an acceptance symbolized by the two women.

Human sexuality is *teleological*; it has a goal and that goal is union
with God. It is only to minds inured to the banal, adolescent pap of
the American fascination with breasts, vulva, phallus, and anus that
could think that eros is satisfied by a mutual orgasm. In most of the recounting of sexual exploits in our contemporary literature the inability of any act of sexual intercourse to capture the bliss of togetherness
it anticipates is ignored. The sadness that follows coitus is, if you will,
an eschatological sign of which poets and philosophers have known
for centuries. Its absence from this culture's infatuation with vivid descriptions of sexual conquest is more than regrettable; it is a sign of
our vapidity.

Whenever eros comes to concrete expression there is to our longing that which is left unexpressed: a surd. Coitus is set within marriage,
and husband and wife become parents, and parents give themselves to
the education of their children. In this regard I was struck by what one
of the respondents said. He spoke of the analogue of "intimate inno-
cency" between his relationship with his wife and his relationship with
God; and then continued saying, "I really enjoy my children. Out of
[my sexual relationship with my wife] has emerged two children that I

enjoy so much. The relationship with God when it is really intimate produces the same kind of children in terms of fruit that comes from that [innocent intimacy]." As I see it, he was grappling with the principle of the surd.

There is a movement in sexuality as it finds successive levels of expression, which is drawn forward as we seek to incorporate the surd. Bernard Lonergan, the Canadian philosophical theologian, in a most significant essay entitled "The Finality of Marriage," argues that this presence of the persistent surd is evidence that the goal of human sexuality can only be realized in humankind's union with God. The eros of humanity moves us forward, but pure longing for the other can only be fulfilled in the redemptive *agapē* of God.

Some psychologists have argued that coitus is at heart an act of anger and violence caused by the male resentment of the female. Like many psychological theories, this notion of an efficient cause for sexual intercourse has an element of truth, but it is also myopic and reductionist. The sexual experience, both in its explicit genital expression and in the more implicit life together, is also a quest for paradise. In the same manner, our longing for God has motivation that lies in our need for assurance of ourselves as we are now, if not also in the plea for divine "goodies," but at its best it is the consuming desire for a more perfect future. "This truly is the vision of God: never to be satisfied in the desire to see him."[3]

When as Christians we see the crucified Christ we know that this same Jesus was raised from the grave as the first fruits of the dead. When as Christians we think of sexuality expressed in an unqualified commitment of man and woman we think of the sign of the love and fidelity of the God who gave his son that we might have life. The priest's dream could point in but one direction, to the oneness that is known when God's love meets our longing for him. In the midst of his pain, he dreamed a dream full of promise.

Body and Spirit

An ordained woman with whom I have discussed the issue of sexuality and prayer has spoken of her own experience. She is a person of long and intense spiritual discipline, which has borne fruit in her own insight and compassion. She has known more than the usual pain of a late-twentieth-century woman and this has swept her heart clean of most romantic illusions. She has described nights spent in prayer, lying in her bed, when she has been overcome by sexual passion. The experience of erotic longing is not for her a deflection away from the subject of her prayer (i.e., God), but a normal and natural concomitant of it.

This experience of sexual passion in prayer is neither new nor surprising. It is difficult to take a poll on such matters, but erotic fantasies come to our minds very naturally in the liturgy for reasons readily explained. Good liturgy taps that same level of our memory wherein lies our sexual imagery. If you stir one you stir the other. I recall with delight a discussion group considering the effects of the ordination of women to the priesthood in the Episcopal Church. One man anxiously asked, "What happens if the woman priest is attractive and I become sexually aroused during the Eucharist?" A woman replied to him, "What do you think has been happening to us for centuries?"

The question raises itself that if human sexuality is a valuable symbol of the human spiritual quest, is it possible to divorce from that symbol the reality of the body? Gregory of Nyssa, who believed firmly in the importance of eros for the spiritual life, was equally firm in wishing to purge eros of all irrational passion. "Every passion is a fall as long as it is passion," he wrote.[4] He was married for a time, but quickly abandoned that estate, describing it as a sad affair. But we know that to be a person is to be an indissoluble union of mind, spirit, emotions, and body. It is not only impossible to purge passion of passion, it is undesirable.

Undoubtedly the union of body and spirit betrays those who might be scandalized to think that their experience of God had a physical correspondence. Yet descriptions of the mystical experience in sexual imagery abound, as well as spiritual words in regard to sexual experiences. Teresa of Avila, a great Christian saint, describes what she calls "rapture" throughout her writings. Teaching her nuns, she saw that God encouraged the soul "to be joined with so great a Lord and to take Him as its Spouse." Having made apologies for this metaphor, she goes on to say:

> And thus you will see what His Majesty does to conclude this betrothal, which I understand must be established when He gives the soul raptures that draw it out of its senses . . . When the kind of rapture is that in which the soul even though not in prayer is touched by some word . . . His Majesty from the

interior of the soul makes the spark we mentioned increase, for he is moved with compassion . . . Now that it [the soul] is so pure, the Lord joins it with Himself, without anyone understanding what is happening except those two.[5]

It is possible to expand on Teresa's imagery at great length. She speaks of rapture as "the flight of the soul," for example, and is fond of describing God as piercing her in the ecstatic experience. Giovanni Lorenzo Bernini (1598–1680) left no doubt as to the sexual connotations of Teresa's spiritual rapture in his famous sculpture of her at such a moment. Her head is tossed back, her eyes closed, and her mouth open in the manner of a woman in orgasm. Over her stands an angelic being, with a dart raised to pierce her soul. The correspondence is obvious.

An experienced spiritual director I consulted in this study described as almost commonplace a conversation with a woman he was directing. She had been in an extended period of solitude and her prayer had reached very deeply into her self. There was a yearning for the Lord, but then, as she put it, "something horrible happened." She discovered that she was sexually aroused. She immediately broke off her prayer. My consultant went on to say that he has subsequently related this vignette and on one occasion a group of nuns confirmed this as their experience as well.

The difficulty we have dealing with the possibility of a physical sexual response in prayer is accentuated by the common perception of particularly male sexuality. Most of the examples I have used here are of women's sexual response. Men are sexually excited as well, but male images of sexual response are a problem for prayer. As already suggested, for men there is a power issue in an erection. It is a way of overcoming the woman, of making a conquest. Inasmuch as God is the lover in the human spiritual experience, it is difficult for the man to conceive of himself as the recipient of the divine solicitation. The passivity that this implies is out of character, which is one reason why men are not as enthusiastic about the prayer life as women. But herein lies a clue to a question that has vexed Christianity for all its history.

Teilhard de Chardin (1881–1955) wrote about the relation between sexuality and spirituality when he discussed chastity as a principle in defense of virginity. He pointed out that for most of its history the church has advocated the avoidance of genital relationships because of its fear of the formidable force of the feminine. The feminine was seen as destructive and disintegrating by men, who have been those making the rules. In the quest for spiritual growth one eschewed matter. Teilhard's reply to this was that in playing it safe Christians have lost a profound enrichment of love that can come through "participation [in the feminine] and conquest."[6] He recognized the problem, but his solution is still a masculine one and he still identifies spirit with a masculine rationality.

Gerald May, a psychiatrist, has studied the relationship between human sexuality and spirituality in considerable detail. He and Teilhard apparently agree that the basic difference between genital union and spiritual union is that the former constitutes a loss. May says, according to Tilden Edwards, that in sexual experience the "world falls away." Teilhard says that a "'short-circuit' is produced . . . a flash which burns up and deadens a portion of the soul." In the spiritual experience "the world arises," according to May. Teilhard says there is a "convergence at a higher level."[7]

The argument is inevitably in part *ad hominem*. For some people the world may well "fan away" at the moment of orgasm. I expect that others would testify that it "arises." I know of no one who would complain of a "deadened soul" after intercourse. I do not say this in jest. But in an attempt to get some distance on the problem, I would say that both Teilhard and Gerald May value a masculine more than a feminine imagery. I believe that the relationship of sexuality to spirituality is better defined where the masculine and feminine images are equally valued and held in a tension that generates an energy that can draw us closer to God.

If David Bohm is correct that matter and consciousness are two forms of energy, then the issue is how they may be joined as expressions of energy to move us toward God, not how consciousness can "master"matter. Teilhard himself writes:

> Rightly speaking, there are no sacred or profane things, no pure or impure: there is only *a good direction and bad direction*—the direction of ascent, of amplifying unity, of greatest spiritual effort; and the direction of descent, of constricting egoism, of materializing enjoyment.[8]

It is my own conviction that in the oscillation between a masculine and feminine consciousness, deeply known in the *total* sexual experience—that is, courtship, foreplay, penetration/reception, orgasm, and postlude—we find ourselves called forward into the experience of divine union.

Merton speaks to this when he as a monk points out that virginity is an absurdity. While this may be a literary overstatement on Merton's part, it can still be argued that man and woman together, expressed in their physical compenetration, make one complete person in a manner that no other interpersonal relationship can fulfill. Rollo May, Gerald May's brother, says that the height of coitus is not orgasm as much as it is the penis entering the vagina. This is saying much the same thing as Merton, in that sexual intercourse can, as it does in my experience, become a sacrament of the coinherence—the bearing of one another's suffering—of God and humanity and of one person to another. The sublimity is in the joining of the bodies of two persons willing to "sift" that experience that it might become an occasion of spiritual enlargement.

Merton describes this when he speaks of the loneliness of the celibate, but then he goes on to speak of the loneliness of the genitally active person as well.

> I can say bluntly that to exist as a man without relating to one particular woman-and-person who is "my love" is quite simply a kind of death. But I have enough experience of human love to realize, too, that even within the best of relationships between man and woman this loneliness and death are also terribly present. There are moments in human love in which loneliness is completely transcended, but these are brief and deceptive, and they can point only to the further and more difficult place where, ultimately, two lonely and helpless persons elect to save one another from absurdity by being absurd together—and for life.[9]

Eros is a tragic gift in its every aspect. To reduce it to venereal games, as our culture does, does not avoid the fact that love leads to death, it only demonically masks the reality. The only resolution of our passion is the love of God; but our passion properly understood—be we celibate, or married—leads us to a death and beyond to resurrection.

I would move beyond Gerald May's argument that there is a profound difference between sexuality and spirituality to suggest that passion's need to possess the other to lose the world can and should be redeemed. There is grace in a woman's moistened vagina and a man's erect penis, if we are willing for that physical delight to become a means of divine presence. This is not a divine presence that we conjure up by thinking about it at the moment of orgasm; although one priest reported to me that on the occasion of first having intercourse with his wife, at the point of orgasm the words of the *Te Deum* suddenly leapt to his mind. Planning intercourse as we plan a liturgy is a kind of Puritan compulsivity that we need to avoid. A sense of the divine presence comes from living our entire life spontaneously around and upon the altar. Why should the intention to make love in the presence of God be anything but a "turn on"? If there is a problem, the problem is ours.

Conclusion

Nancy Van Scoyoc in *Women, Change, and the Church*[10] reports that women in the church today feel comfortable sharing with their pastors problems of illness, death, and parenting and family concerns, but among those matters they do not readily share are issues of sexuality. My hunch is that this is because clergy as a whole "talk a good game," speaking freely of sexual behavior, but that we have not integrated the meaning of our own sexuality into our own lives.

I think there are three reasons for the difficult integration of sexuality, including genital relations, into our spirituality. First and most fundamental, our culture and especially our religious symbolism does not sanction an *overt* feminine consciousness in males. There is an old rabbinic saying, which is true, to the effect that women are religious, but men have to learn to be religious. Christianity—particularly Christianity that is suspicious of the cult of the Blessed Virgin or is insensitive to the Holy Spirit as Sophia—is a very masculine religion. But if we are to understand the finality of human sexuality in God, then the male will have to share with the female in a participation in the feminine dimension of the sexual relationship.

Second, we are not comfortable with our bodies, despite all bravado to the contrary. The historic Puritan mistrust of the body should be taken seriously to the extent that physical desire, left to its own devices, leads nowhere but to disintegration of the self. But an eviscerated spirituality lacks an earthiness that is necessary for the redemption of the whole person. It becomes unreal.

Third, the expectation that overt sexuality, not necessarily including genital intercourse, will and must be fulfilled in a monogamous, lifelong marriage, and that all relationships outside marriage are either asexual or only implicitly sexual is not only naive, it is self-defeating. It creates the illusion that there is a perfect, divine marriage, in which both partners are totally fulfilled before God in the other. This is contrary to universal experience. It also obscures a special kind of sexual relationship, which by definition is nongenital, but of a profoundly transcendent quality. This kind of relationship may well lie behind the dream with which I opened this chapter.

III. The Context

7. Worship and Spirituality

IN THE previous three chapters I have explored the contemporary meaning of the evangelical counsels of obedience, poverty, and chastity. In this chapter and the two that follow the subject is the context of spirituality in the church's worship, in the unconscious, and in the pastor's life in the parish.

The late Middle Ages have often been blamed for perversions in the history of Christian thought that the Reformation set straight—be it the Protestant, Anglican, or Roman Reformation. Doubtless the sixteenth century was one of those great pivotal periods in our history, much like the fourth and twelfth centuries; but there was not as radical a discontinuity with the fourteenth and fifteenth centuries as some might think. Many of the strengths and weaknesses of modern Western Christianity find their roots in the late Middle Ages. Among the weaknesses is the split between personal piety and liturgical prayer, which still pesters the church despite our efforts in the last several generations to deal with it.

As early as the twelfth century medieval piety began to focus on the humanity of our Lord and personal relationship with him. The Franciscans in the thirteenth century did much to foster this infatuation with the individual's relation to the Jesus of history. This ran from a fondness for the Christmas crib to a vivid recollection of the crucifixion. A personal mysticism emerged, engendered by numerous pious communities that arose in the late thirteenth, fourteenth, and fifteenth centuries (e.g., the Beguines, the Beghards, and the Friends of God). An early leader in the Beguine movement, Hadewijch, imagined herself addressed by the human Jesus in these words: "If you wish to be like me in my humanity . . . you shall desire to be poor, miserable, and despised by all men."[1] The goal of devotion became the imitation of Christ. It is for this reason and perhaps for none other that the principal work of popular fifteenth-century devotion by Thomas à Kempis (c.1380–471) was called *The Imitation of Christ.* The piety of this period is known as the *devotio moderna* ("modern devotion") and was in the tradition of Hadewijch, Jan van Ruysbroeck (1293–1381), who was profoundly influenced by her writings, and the author of the *Theologica Germanica* (c.1350), which Martin Luther so greatly admired. *The Imitation of Christ* is in the judgment of many scholars a second-rate piece of work.

The personal piety of the *devotio moderna* was characteristic of persons who were faithful in their attendance at the Eucharist, but for whom the sacrament itself had undergone a change in meaning. Individuals were present at Mass, but rarely communicated. Liturgy was an occasion for a private experience of the Christ; there was no sense of corporate worship. Churches were filled with oratories, where Masses were offered for the departed. Benediction of the Blessed Sacrament, an extra-liturgical devotion that appealed to the sentiment of the individual, had become popular.

Hadewijch relates a vision she had at the Eucharist in which our Lord came and fed her. The language is rife with sexual implications and it is clearly a private meeting of two individuals.

> Then he gave himself to me in the shape of the Sacrament . . .
> After that he came himself to me, took me entirely in his arms,
> and pressed me to him; and all my members felt his in full fe-
> licity, in accordance with the desire of my heart and my hu-
> manity. So I was outwardly satisfied and fully transported.[2]

The Imitation of Christ two hundred years later was a manual for making a good communion, but this good communion is a matter of personal absorption into Jesus. " 'Thou in me, and I in thee'; so also grant that we may both continue together in one."[3]

The Reformation did nothing to change the direction or blunt this heavy focus upon inner feelings. In fact, it built upon it. Louis Bouyer is correct when he writes:

> But Protestantism is much more truly the product of medieval
> piety [than a reaction against it] because it is the fruit of what
> lay in that piety in seed-form: a naturalistic outlook on religion,
> a systematic ignoring of the Mystery, a sentimental kind of re-

ligious "experience" in place of the sober mysticism, completely grounded on faith, of the great Christian tradition.[4]

What he fails to note is that popular Roman Catholic piety was the same.

Johann Arndt (1555–1621), a Lutheran mystic who came to be the spiritual father of Pietism, wrote, "He [Christ] made himself like you so that you might make yourself like him."[5] It sounds like Irenaeus (c.130–200), except the corporate, objective sense has been diminished and it becomes something the individual discovers through a personal relationship within himself. Arndt spoke of communion in the Eucharist as the occasion "which unites and binds us together by a power of faith and the spirit with the Lord Christ out of the true inner affection of love."[6] It is Hadewijch all over again.

It is this personal devotion that shapes the enthusiasm of the Pietists of the late seventeenth century. It was imported to the American colonies and became the first and second Great Awakenings that provided the momentum and shape of the American revivalist tradition. In fact, the acceptance of Jesus Christ as one's personal Lord and Savior is in the minds of many people what the Christian Gospel is about, even when it is not tied to the emotional experience of the consolation sought by the revivalist tradition. The fact that such personal piety is only one possible form of Christian spirituality comes as a surprise to the average believer in the United States—perhaps in Western Christianity—so pervasive has been its viewpoint since the fourteenth and fifteenth centuries.

But there is a deep flaw in the personal piety directed toward the human Jesus, as it comes to us from the Middle Ages and early modern times. It lacks a firm bond with the corporate worship of the church, in particular the two major sacraments of Baptism and the Eucharist. The Reformation debate over the nature of Christ's presence in the elements of the Eucharist is understandable if we are conscious of the desire for a meeting of the individual with the humanity of Christ and the debate that surrounded the degree of objectivity vis-à-vis subjectivity in that encounter. John Macquarrie, a contemporary Anglican theologian, resolves the argument of the nature of Christ's presence by saying that there are three kinds of presence: temporal, local, and personal. Jesus is, as he sees it, really *personally* present in the Eucharist. But what Macquarrie says is easily appropriated only to reinforce a "me-and-thee" eucharistic piety much like that of Hadewijch.

The notion that Christ is personally present to the individual per-

son in the Eucharist and, particularly, in the act of communion, resulted in a eucharistic piety that survived until the middle of this century. One went to "hear Mass." Individual personal devotions,
including saying the rosary, were normal practice while being present
at the Eucharist. The symbol of our corporate presence, the passing of
the peace, became unthinkable (and still is in many places).

When the objective of attendance at the Eucharist as an intimate
tête-à-tête with Jesus was joined to that depressed doctrine of humanity stemming from elaborations on the meaning of original sin em-
phasizing human worthlessness that ran through Western Christianity
from the Black Death to the American frontier, the result was disas-
trous. People came to believe that there were no alternatives in Christian theology but to think of themselves in the words of the *Book of
Common Prayer* (until the 1979 Episcopal version) as "miserable sinners" and were quite willing to sing with enthusiasm gospel hymns
such as "Amazing Grace" in which they described themselves as
"wretches." The grim effect was that communion came to be viewed
as a fearsome thing, not to be engaged in too frequently. In the Roman
Catholic tradition it required careful preparation such as sacramental
confession, fasting from the midnight before, and extensive prepara-
tory, penitential prayers. In traditions where the subjective personal
experience was emphasized as a hedge against a theology of gloom,
the sacrament itself was less and less frequently celebrated in favor of
preaching services calculated to conjure up the feeling of the consolation. More effective ways of evoking pious feelings than a dull observance of the Lord's Supper eventually overrode the obvious biblical
centrality of the Eucharist.

I was struck by an explanation given me by the one ordained person who spoke negatively of the importance of the Eucharist or Lord's
Supper to him. As he explained his attitude, it was that he was "by in-
stinct and conviction a low churchman." He went on to illustrate this
by recounting a story of an elaborate and pointless piece of ceremony
surrounding the taking up of the offering at a church he once visited.
It was as if I were asking him if he preferred his eggs scrambled, hard
or soft. The question of the centrality of the Eucharist, as best I could
tell, was in his understanding a matter of personal taste.

There is very little in our tradition reaching back over five or six
hundred years to encourage a causal connection between corporate
worship and personal prayer. The absurdity of some of our inherited
thinking is only now beginning to dawn on us. There is a growing

sense among most clergy that this dichotomy ought not to exist, a certain feeling that it does not exist for them, and a hope that it will no longer exist among the people they serve.

A Theology of the Sacraments

My soul is cast down within me,
therefore I remember thee
from the land of Jordan and of Hermon,
from Mount Mizar.
Deep calls to deep at the thunder of thy cataracts;
and all thy waves and thy billows
have gone over me.
(Psalm 42:6–7, rsv)

The poetry of the psalmist evokes images that speak to the meaning of the sacraments as they engage the people of God. "Deep calls to deep." God touches us from the depths of his being at the level of our own deep memory. In his sacraments he proclaims the mystery of his presence among us and shapes our awareness at its root.

The sacraments are the central means whereby we participate in the Passion of our Lord. His suffering, death, and resurrection are the paradigm for creation. Out of suffering and even death comes new life. The cross is both an instrument of torture and the revelation of the divine love for all creation. The Passion is the fundamental story of Christian believing, of which everything is an elaboration. As we seek to be open to a relationship with God, to become more aware of what it is to be human, the fundamental piece of history that shapes our total view is the suffering, death, and resurrection of Jesus. It is our personal story, because it is the story of the people of God and the cosmos itself.

There is an objectivity to the Passion that presses itself upon our primordial memory and transcends how I or any other individual might feel about the humanity of Jesus. Bouyer says in his great classic, *Liturgical Piety*, that it would be very wrong to try to suppress the piety of the last seven or eight hundred years. But we need to understand such piety within the much larger setting of the mystery of God as creator. We are made by God to be social beings, with a public life that cannot be separated from our private being. There can be no devotion worthy of the name Christian that does not challenge our life in the streets.

The Passion judges my sentiment and calls me to faith in the midst of affliction, when the last thing I am inclined to do is to believe in a God who loves me. By virtue of its objectivity I am no longer the victim, the prisoner, of my pious emotions. "Called or not called, God is there" *in spite of how I feel.* He is there in the stark historical reality of the agony of the cross and in the wonder of Easter. It is that crucified/risen presence that in the sacraments—but particularly the great sacraments of Baptism and Eucharist—embeds itself deep within my memory to withstand the challenges of the sceptical, the clever sayings of the cynical, and saccharine promises of the sentimental.

A ritual is a weaving together of those symbols into a significant whole, which, as the church repeats the ritual again and again, makes us present as participants in that event that called our community into being. This making present—*anamnesis* is the technical word—penetrates our deep meaning with the power of the event. It is not that we summon up Christ's presence as Saul did Samuel (1 Sam. 28:3–20). Rather it is that by virtue of the sacraments we become vulnerable at the deepest level to that divine mind that transcends time and space and is always present.

The earliest account we have of the institution of the Eucharist is from Paul. According to this account our Lord told us to eat his flesh and drink his blood "for the purpose of my re-presentation" (1 Cor. 11:24). What is made present to our consciousness at some level is not just the humanity of Jesus, but the reality of God's son, who suffered, died, and rose. It is this event that gave birth to the Christian church.

In similar fashion Paul tells us that in baptism we are buried with Christ and lie dead, so that we might be raised to a new life (Rom. 6:4). The death and resurrection of our Lord become an indelible part of our memories, shaping our understanding of the world, by virtue of our baptism. It is this awareness that becomes the script by which the Christian saint lives out his life. Death cannot destroy him. He has already died and been raised with Christ and only awaits the time of glorification when he becomes united with God.

The sacraments are a window into a cosmic drama. They are the means by which we become formed as characters in that tragic comedy of the Passion. Our spirituality is set within this corporate performance and given an objectivity that frames our subjective imagination and shapes it according to the divine vision, while giving it freedom to improvise for itself. The prayer of the sacraments becomes a reality through time and space that unites with our own quest and provides a depth of authenticity that no mere sentiment can plumb. It is not our feelings alone that become those of Christ crucified and risen, it is our entire person, its history and its community. We are a people who are to pray the Passion as naturally as we eat, sleep, or copulate.

Of course, the Holy Scriptures are integral to this understanding of the sacraments. On the surface the division of Word and Sacrament makes sense, but experientially it does not. They are experienced as one. The story of the Bible is enacted in sensible (i.e., pertaining to the five senses) form in liturgy. Word and Sacrament are interwoven so that while the integrity of both is preserved, they engage the people of God as one and are buried in their memory as one.

It is my belief that people at heart are the shape of the images within their deep memory. It is in terms of these images that they make basic sense of their experience and it is for whatever values these may evoke that they will die. Christian spirituality is rightly the shape of Baptism and Eucharist. In the latter Christ *took, broke, blessed,* and *gave.* Our spirituality is a taking of life, an acceptance of its brokenness, a giving thanks for its gift, and a sharing of it with others. This is particularly, but not exclusively, true for the priest or pastor.

André Louf, a French Trappist monk, has described the relationship of the liturgy to the spiritual life, drawing upon an early fourth-century Syriac writing called *The Book of Degrees.* The life of prayer begins, he says, with the visible liturgy in the church. This liturgy, however, is internalized by the liturgy of the heart deep within the memory of the worshiper. Finally, there is the celestial liturgy, by which Louf implies that the visible liturgy of the church is a reflection of eternal order within the cosmos. The liturgy within the heart stands midway between the visible liturgy of the church and the celestial liturgy. What Louf is suggesting is that there needs to be congruity between the symbolic reality of the church's ritual, the inner disposition of the worshiper, and the mind of God. There is a shaping that takes place that conforms us in the liturgy to the divine intention.

William of St. Thierry (c.1085–1148) spoke of this relationship by using the traditional language of sacramental theology. The *sacramentum,* the thing signifying, is the external or visible liturgy. The *res,* the thing signified, is the internal disposition of the worshiper. In the liturgy we celebrate the death and resurrection of Christ as it is em-

bedded within ourselves and becomes the primordial image by means
of which all else in life is understood.

The Place of the Eucharist

There is a consensus that is emerging in classical Christianity as to the
importance of the Eucharist. Certainly in the various ecumenical dia-
logues going on these days there is little problem in drawing up statements of agreement on sacramental theology, be we Roman Catholics,
Anglicans, Lutherans, Methodists, or Presbyterians. This impression of
near unanimity was reinforced by those interviewed when asked what
value they placed upon the Eucharist in their own piety.

A Lutheran pastor commented that for him the Eucharist

> is essential. It's on an equal plane with the preaching ministry,
> with the Gospel. So far as I'm concerned it's necessary for the
> life of the church. [In] the development in America one of the
> problems has been the emphasis on the big preacher, and very
> little emphasis on the sacrament.

Another Lutheran described the importance of the Eucharist for him
as "quite high." He went on to explain, speaking of himself and his
people, "We take quite literally the belief of the church in terms of the
real presence, and that goes with our understanding of spirituality."

It is no surprise that a Roman Catholic priest said, "The essential
place of the Mass is being the life stream of the church and in being
the life stream of each individual member." The interesting thing is
that he spoke with the same voice as everyone else. A Methodist pastor said, "I find the liturgy catches us up in the faith and allows us to
live the faith."

Two Episcopal priests used the same images. It is "in the center"
of their piety, although it is interesting that one very slight demurral
came from another Episcopal priest. "Just purely from a gut level," he
said, "[The Eucharist] is not as important [to my piety] as silence and
private prayer, but I am lost when I cannot take part in it on a regular
basis. It's sort of like a regular meal I appreciate subtly." This particular person placed a very high priority upon the inner journey. He had
invested a great deal of time and effort in being under spiritual direction, and this was reflected in his attitude.

The following statement by a Presbyterian pastor both expressed his agreement with the general outlook of those interviewed and also raised a point made simultaneously by a number of persons. In response to the question of the importance of the Eucharist to him, he replied:

It was an incredibly meaningful thing to me the first time I served the Lord's Supper. That's mysterious. I'm probably pretty much where John Calvin differed from Zwingli in Zwingli thinking of it as a remembrance. He [Calvin] said that more was going on there than just a remembrance. It was mainly something God was doing. It is very meaningful to me. I would like to serve it more often.

Aside from his awareness with Calvin of remembrance as representation, the question of the frequency of celebration of the Eucharist is worth noting. Obviously this is not an issue for Roman Catholics, although the regularity of attendance certainly is. But for one Episcopalian I interviewed and for several Protestants the question of how often a congregation celebrates the Eucharist arose naturally. Frequency was related to importance, but there was a fear of too frequent a celebration becoming a banal observance. There was a tendency to see the Eucharist as needing to be a part of some emotionally compelling experience. The church needs to examine this latest equation of effective worship to an emotional charge.

The matter of frequency needs to be seen in relation to another issue that I discussed with a number of clergy. Most of those interviewed believed that they placed higher value on the Eucharist than the people they served did. The reason often given for this was our cultural impoverishment in Western Christianity. It did not matter what the denominational allegiance was, they agreed that people have not been socialized to think symbolically. For most of the priests and pastors the recovery of the meaning of the Eucharist has been a process that transcends the collective consciousness of our society. They have found ways to explore their own inner meaning at some depth from resources not generally available to the populace. Most people in the pews have little awareness of their deep memory and the images embedded in that memory.

In our society we have for centuries valued the objectification of reality for the sake of control and prediction. We have concentrated our thinking on the appearances and not on the inner meaning so that we might manipulate an "objective reality" without raising the question of its meaning and our recognition that this "reality" is of our own making and does not exist apart from the collective subject that has constructed it. For this reason, we quickly conclude that people who live different realities are "crazy" or even "evil."

What has been sacrificed to the values of control and prediction is imagination and intuition. For example, when a school budget is cut, what goes first? Those courses that relate to the imagination: art, music, and dance. What gets funding most readily in higher education? Certainly not the curriculum that exists for its own sake, with no identifiable, immediate payoff in the "practical world." There are exceptions but not enough of them to correct an endemic retardation of the imagination among the general population.

Yet sacramental theology in particular and prayer in general does not thrive on the illusion of an objective reality that we think we can control and predict. Both draw on a symbolic reality, requiring persons with a sophisticated imagination that enables us to feed from and to use the symbolic images deep within our memories. No matter what society, claims, those images are there; it is a matter of living with them *intentionally*. It is to this need that the ordained persons in this study spoke with concern.

It is my own conviction that one does not tap the world of symbolic reality by occasional trips into that universe with the expectation of a profoundly moving experience on each such occasion. This seems analogous to an expectation that beginning on the wedding night a married couple may rightfully expect a marvelous mutual orgasm and that everything is downhill from then on, just so long as they do not overdo it. The sexual knowledge of one's spouse is a road of valleys, plateaus, and peaks, and only by traveling that road with frequency and commitment does one come to a deep awareness of the other. This is even more true of participation in the Eucharist.

It is not the task of this study to argue for a specific congregational practice, although it would be disingenuous of me not to admit a conviction that Sunday worship should invariably be the Eucharist with sermon. It is to contend that for the pastor and his or her people spirituality is rooted in a mature experience of the sacramental life. In this instance familiarity does not breed contempt, it forms the person in the shape of Baptism and Eucharist where it counts: deep within the memory. It is an issue of how best we are formed by eucharistic prayer; and I contend it is by the regular weekly, perhaps even daily, presence at the symbolic offering with Christ of his one, sufficient sacrifice.

As a way of illustrating this point it helps to remember that the argument for the communion of little children—say age three to seven—is that they have by this time a developed imagination, which is not buried beneath layers of logical explanation of the world. The rational capacity of the mind comes later (fully at chronological age fourteen), and while it is not entirely necessary, there is an advantage in engaging the deep, intuitive capacity of the memory while it is vulnerable. Once the sacramental images find their place at this deep level, they are there for good. This is why religious educators are more and more aware that if they are given the care of very young children in a sacramental setting, the assurance of their persistence in the faith is greatly increased.

Praying Our Baptism

Martin Luther had inscribed on the wall of his study in Latin the words: "I have been baptized." This constant reminder was for him the assurance of identity in Christ in the face of death. But this identity is not something we wear like a "Celebrate Life" button; if it were a thing to be worn it would be more like a shroud.

Luther himself was a son of that fifteenth-century piety that celebrated the *Totentanz*, the Dance of Death. In this medieval allegory Death, often depicted as a skeleton, meets persons in various walks of life and leads them to the grave. In Ingmar Bergman's great film *The Seventh Seal*, the story is woven around the Dance of Death. The title of the film is from the Revelation of St. John the Elder, the seventh seal being the final consummation of history. "Now when the Lamb broke the seventh seal, there was silence in heaven for what seemed half an hour" (Rev. 8:1). The story of Bergman's film takes place in the late Middle Ages when the Black Death swept Europe. It is a study of the way in which we face death; it is the breaking of the seventh seal for each individual.

Baptism is the way the Christian anticipates the silence in heaven. The symbolism of baptism is built around the image of death. It is greatly to be regretted that in classical Christian baptismal practice total immersion or the descent into the pool in the baptistry has almost entirely disappeared. These actions capture the symbolism of baptism as a burial of one who has died to everything that denies God's creative purpose and joins his or her death with Christ's suffering, death, and burial.

"Already at our birth," says Gregory of Nyssa, "we are driven by the very nature of things toward our departure, for which we must carefully prepare our hands, feet, and the rest."[7] Gregory the Great (c.540–604) said that all of life is a *prefixitas mortis*, "death drawn out." Seneca (4 b.c.–65 a.d.) said that when we start to live we begin to die. The question is not whether we shall die, but how we shall die. According to John Donne, to live as if we shall not die is a form of atheism.

> Death I recant, and say, unsaid by mee
> What ere hath slip'd, that might diminish thee.
> Spiritual treason, atheisme 'tis, to say,
> That any can thy Summons disobey.[8]

As suggested by both Gregory and Donne it is characteristic of the spiritual masters to meditate upon their death. Donne perhaps took it to extremes when he was seriously ill in 1623, having himself painted in his shroud and coffin.

There is nothing heroic about a corpse. The circumstances of a death might be considered exemplary, but the physical fact of dying, George Herbert reminded us, is the demise of vitality.

> Death, thou wast once an uncouth hideous thing,
> Nothing but bones,
> The sad effect of sadder grones:
> Thy mouth was open, but thou couldst not sing.[9]

Death is our becoming nothing. We pass under the water, we disappear into the grave, and all that was beauty and life is gone.

> For we consider'd thee as some six
> Or ten years hence;
> After the losse of life and sense,
> Flesh being turned to dust, and bones to sticks.[10]

The message of our baptism, however, is that just when we have become the hideous nothing, the possibility of new life begins. This is not a temporal sequence, but an existential reality. No one can perceive the crucifixion of Jesus in its true light unless he or she looks at it through the awareness of his or her own death. A priest spoke to me of his own new realization. He was sitting in his shop—he is a skilled craftsman—when suddenly it came to him that he had to die and that all this around him, his house, the beautiful things he makes, even his family, would be as nothing to him. Then the Gospel seemed to come alive.

I scattered the ashes of a man upon the lawn of a house, a man with whom a few weeks before I had shared a drink in that same house. What does it mean? All is vanity? There is more to the grave than dust and ashes if we are to be raised with the Lord with whom we have also been buried. As again Herbert writes of death:

> But since our Saviour's death did put some bloud
> Into thy face;
> Thou art grown fair and full of grace,
> Much in request, much sought for as good.[11]

When seen in terms of the cross of Christ, which we in our baptism have embraced, death takes on a new demeanor. It is not only an end, it is a new beginning. It is no less brutal, but there is a way beyond.

The rhetoric of a Christian death may strike many people in our age as strange, if not empty. But my own experience with priests and pastors, as well as lay persons, is to the contrary. Early in my ordained ministry a simple woman with no more than a third-grade education told me after a sermon in which I suggested everyone rightly fears death that she herself did not. It was not said in refutation as much as a reaching out to me in my young, naive cynicism. A woman priest interviewed for this study said that she looks forward to dying. This is a beautiful woman, who enjoys her good looks, her family, and the world around her. Yet death is for her "much in request, much sought for as good." Anyone who thinks that these two people suffer from some deep neurosis has been seduced by the spirit of our present age. They exemplify the Christian who thinks, as one rightly should, about his or her death.

Of those persons interviewed, on the mean they said that they occasionally look forward to dying and being with Jesus (2.93 on a scale of 1 to 5, n = 15). They feel abandoned by God almost as frequently (2.67 on a scale of 1 to 5, n = 15). However, prayer is for them only rarely an experience of dying (1.67 on a scale of 1 to 5, n = 15). The spread on the response to the first question, however, ran from 1 to 5.

There is a tentativeness that surrounds the image of death. It is to this tentativeness that prayer in the spirit of our baptism may speak. We are to the world of Satan as men and women already dead, but to God as citizens of his Kingdom.

When I was first ordained I had a good friend who was a priest in a nearby town. He was a young man full of promise—the kind who seemed born to the ordained ministry. Handsome, articulate, personable, he quickly gained greater responsibility. In his mid-thirties he became rector of the largest parish in his diocese, and then a fatal flaw appeared. Marital and family troubles, alcoholism, and a near fatal automobile accident characterized a misfortune that hounded him from parish to parish, until in despair he sought secular employment. He became the district manager of a chain of small rural stores. One Sunday while he was helping a local proprietor with his inventory, three men came to the store, robbed them, and then senselessly murdered my friend and his companions.

I reflect from time to time upon my friend's death. His was not the road nor the end I would want. When I tell his story I find that people frequently try to soften the dread it evokes. We would all prefer that the joyous words that Bonaventure (1221–1274) wrote of the death of Francis of Assisi be said of us.

> His body was so much in harmony with his spirit and so ready to obey it that, when he strove to attain complete holiness, his body not only did not resist, but often tried to run ahead.[12]

But somehow my friend's death, appearing to lie at the opposite pole, may be more familiar to us. I do not know if he died in bitterness or hope. Surely he must have felt that same abandonment that came to our Lord upon the cross. To the world his death was simply tragic. In the light of his and our baptism we may pray that it was an offering in death, of a life already broken in service and by God's infinite mercy made perfect.

Praying the Eucharist

Perhaps the most erotic scene I recall in a movie was in *Tom Jones*, a picture released before the explicit sex films of the current era. *Tom*

Jones would probably rate a "PG" now. Set in the bawdy eighteenth century, the movie is packed with innuendo. On one occasion Tom and his opposite number are eating in a tavern, the meal laid before them. Particularly memorable is the eating of a bunch of grapes. Oral gratification and, by implication, sexual fulfillment are joined in one great celebration.

To "eat" someone is a vulgarism for oral sexual play, but is not without deeper meaning. It suggests that common identification of digestion with copulation as modes of assimilation.

The Eucharist is a sacrament of oral incorporation. It is an action expressed in the mode of the senses: touch, seeing, hearing, taste, and smell. The human person incorporates the other sensually—be it food or a person. In the act of communion the person of the risen Lord becomes our food. By eating and drinking the body and blood we become Christ. All that our Lord represents is incorporated into our way of building a world and being in the world . . . sensually.

Among some devout people the earthly language of sacramental theology is too strong. The authentic religious experience must be spiritual, by which they mean noncorporeal or nonmolecular. The physical world fails, because it is not supernatural. The fear of the chthonic inspires a puritanism that pervades almost every world religion. It begets a cosmic dualism, sometimes to the point of identifying evil with matter.

I know a woman who will not make her communion because, as she explains, it smacks of cannibalism. Without doubt she has her co-thinkers throughout the church. The Romans accused the Christians of being cannibals because they ate the flesh and drank the blood of Jesus. If one must make a choice, it is better to plead guilty to the charge of cannibalism than to assure people that we only speak of the body and blood of Christ in a "spiritual" (i.e., unreal) sense. If we lose the sensual meaning of the Eucharist, the scandal and the hope it provokes slip from our faith.

For Christianity is a religion of the Incarnation. God became man in every sense, except he did not sin. This so-called scandal of particularity is the glory of Christian belief. Sometimes we forget that God was in Christ as a sexual, sensual, eating, and drinking person. The attempt to remove the guts of our religion leads to the inescapable conclusion that God did not truly become human and that his creation is not altogether his own. What is wrong with acknowledging, for example, that while there is no way of knowing what Jesus' sex life might

have been, we do believe that as a human he had sexual desires? Is this
any different from reading of his thirst or his fatigue?

The Eucharist as an act of eating and drinking of the sacramental
body and blood of Christ is a means of incorporation. It has sexual
connotations which should be acknowledged and made explicit. This
is consistent with the Incarnation. In the Eucharist we declare our love
for Christ and our desire to be one with him just as in sexual intercourse we declare our expressed longing for the other and consum-
mate that union. In this way our prayer consecrates our sensual nature
and lifts our total being to God.

That remarkable woman, Julian of Norwich, writes somewhat enigmatically:

> God wants us to understand and believe that we are more
> truly in heaven than on earth. Our faith comes from the nat-
> ural love of our soul, and from the clear light of our reason,
> and from the steadfast memory which we have from God, in
> our first creation . . . So I understand that our sensuality is
> founded in nature, in mercy and in grace, and this founda-
> tion enables us to receive gifts which lead us to endless life.[13]

Julian seems to argue that there is a congruence that links the love that
springs from sensual stimulation to the intuition of God and in turn to
the grace of the divine presence that binds us to him. To pray the Eucharist is to know this congruence between the physical incorporation
of the other, our restless search for God, and the sober inebriation that
comes in realizing that the Christ is in us as one whom we eat and
drink daily. He is our daily bread.

Conclusion

Prayer is a way of seeing. There are two components to an act of seeing. We look in a certain direction and we look through a lens, as in the
lens of the eye. What we see depends on both these elements: our direction and our focus (the shape of our lens). In prayer we look in and
through ourselves to God and through him to the world. But the point
of this chapter is that the lens that shapes our seeing at a rudimentary
level is the church's worship, the liturgy of Baptism and the Eucharist.

This is what keeps the prayer of the individual from becoming
merely eccentric and consequently narcissistic. The evaluation of the

spiritual life rests on its grounding or lack of grounding in the sacraments. If certain Christians feel themselves at odds with the symbolic reality of Baptism and Eucharist the problem lies with them. The judgment rests upon those individuals and the church needs to make no stronger case for a surrender of their pride to the tradition.

8. Prayer and the Unconscious

CHRISTIAN prayer emerges from the worship of the church. It is also an expression of an individual's unconscious. When the church possesses a rich symbolic life that stirs the deep memory of its people, then a person's own inner life is drawn into consciousness and becomes available to him or her in an unself-conscious manner. At those times like our own, however, when in fact the church is insensitive to if not terrified of the symbolic world, the formation of the bridge between our life of prayer and our own unconscious becomes the task of each individual. This is particularly the responsibility of the ordained person, not only for his or her own sake, but in the hope that the vapidity of the church's spiritual life and teaching might be overcome.

One criticism leveled at this study that arose during the research was that my premises are "intellectual." The challenger spoke for a great many people who think of the spiritual life as the experience of being addressed by the Word of God without any active intervention upon the part of the person so addressed. In this view one comes to the Scriptures as a spiritual individual, prepared to hear what the Holy Spirit is saying, with the assumption that this word is unmediated by the active history of the hearer. Contrary to the traditional position of my own Anglican heritage, the authority of the Scriptures requires no other qualification such as tradition and, in particular, the reason of the community and individual.

My challenger was quite right. My approach is intellectual in that the human mind cannot know without interpreting. Interpretation is the active intervention—either skilled or unskilled—of the mind. The mind operates not only at the level of reason, but also by means of common sense, intuition, and feeling. Any other assumption is, in all char-

121

ity, naive. The Bible itself is clear evidence of this process. For example, the four Gospel accounts, Matthew, Mark, Luke, and John, are the work of a number of authors and editors who have left the stamp of their particular history and its interpretation of Christ upon the experience of Jesus or, if they were not eyewitnesses, upon the tradition passed on to them. Their obvious differences are a result of these different histories.

This is not to say there is no value in reading the Scriptures with an open mind and heart and letting the words flow into our being. Quite to the contrary; all the respondents to the study testified to the absolute necessity of grounding our spirituality in the Bible. But there is a need to be aware of the self in relation to what we hear, so that what we read can better enter into dialogue with our own history and the inevitable bias it begets. In this way we do not give undue weight to opinions that are formed in hearing the Bible and permit them to tyrannize us and, much worse, others.

The possibility of knowing God pertains to the operation of the mind. This function is a process drawing upon its own content. The mind works analytically and imaginatively, as well as instinctively. It draws on the various images embedded at different levels within our memory, in dialogue with the environment that confronts us in order to make sense of our experience. This process and this content are both the condition of and the instrument in the spiritual growth of the person. We know the presence of God by our deepened awareness of him in our world. The act of thinking in itself is the point of meeting between God and humanity. Furthermore, the shaping of our thoughts by our own unique memories, even as we think in the act of reading the Bible, is what gives a pattern to our awareness that is inevitably our own.

If one traces the process of thinking that operates within the memory of each person back through its different levels of images, one can ultimately stand before the primordial abyss that lies within each of us and through which God speaks. The memory is like a cylinder, open at either end, with layers of memory stacked like a parfait within the cylinder. At the upper end is the mind's engagement with our everyday experience. At the lower end there is only the energy of God impinging upon our memory at its deepest, that same energy that David Bohm argues is the fundamental source of matter and consciousness. In a sense, our memory has a bottom and that bottom is the mystery of divine creativity, waiting to be known—a power that is yet to us a cipher. Yet that bottom is what sustains us.

It is important to note in passing why I speak of the energy of God, rather than God himself. I believe that Gregory Palamas (c.1296–1359), the Byzantine theologian and spiritual guide, was right: we do not know God in his essence, but we know him in his uncreated energy. The essence we attribute to divine being is the "clothing" our minds place upon the divine energy drawn from our finite memory and environment. When we predict a "whatness" to God—for example, God is good—it is always infinitely qualified. He is good as we know the idea of "good," but infinitely more. In fact, as the *via negativa* (negative way) in theology teaches, God is good only as contrasted with the statement: God is *not* good. This concept has widespread implications for this study and particularly for this chapter.

I have been told the sad yet heartening story of a seminary teacher I knew some years ago. When his son died tragically, he left the campus for a period. Upon his return, he appeared unexpectedly at a seminary dinner and spoke to those gathered. "Ladies and gentlemen," he said, "in the last few weeks I have been to the bottom. But I am happy to report that the bottom is solid." It is this bottom of which I speak, in which we come to know the creative energy of God. This chapter is a discussion of how we reach that bottom intentionally and consistently.

But first I would return to my challenger. The reading of the Scriptures is an act of coming face-to-face with the mystery of God, out of which we are addressed. This follows from the fact that Scriptures are the memory of the church. It is as we enter into dialogue between the church's memory and our own memory and make the former our own at an even deeper level of our personal memory that we eventually stand before the mystery of God's presence. The Scriptures are not simply an external authority. Their power arises from their internal appropriation by the mind so that they might enrich our memory and draw us deeper into the process of discerning God's vision for us.

In this sense the Scriptures are poetry, because poetry is the language of the deep memory. This statement runs the clear risk of being immediately misunderstood; for in our culture we are often inclined to dismiss something as "only poetry," just as we discount the opinion of another person by saying she is "only imagining it." This negative evaluation of poetry and the imagination is the contemporary illusion. The imagination is vital to our spiritual growth and poetry is fundamental to our awareness of the experience of God. It is true that poetry raises more questions than it provides answers for, but this is what we should expect from the Scriptures. Read as poetry they draw us ever deeper into the mystery of who God is.

The relation between the corporate scriptural memory and the personal memory at the heart of the movement into the mind of God is similar to what the medieval spiritual masters meant by the anagogical method of scriptural interpretation. There are four ways to interpret Scripture, according to their understanding: the historical or literal sense (which is of the least value), the tropological or moral sense, the allegorical, and the anagogical. The anagogical interpretation of Scripture looks for the hidden meanings that illumine our true end, that is, what God's intention is for us. This is done by attending to those symbols in the Bible that lead us beyond the literal, moral, or allegorical meaning to where we may be addressed by the mystery. The goal is a true wisdom. By implication the divine will in its pure form lies beneath the historical expression of Scripture, which is constituted out of the church's memory.

Just as the Scriptures provide one pole of the dialogue between personal and corporate memory, so do the sacraments offer a "marinade" for the self which develops a congruence between the inner person and his or her life in the community of Christ. We have discussed this in the previous chapter. My purpose here is only to remind us that certain seemingly inborn archetypal images relating to birth and death, sexuality, healing, and wholeness are picked up and restated in the church's sacraments. The power of our liturgy comes from the connection made between the memory of the individual participants and the representation of the Passion by means of the ritual symbols.

It is then in Word and Sacrament that in this interrelated fashion the individual's memory is undergirded by the divine will perceived in its pure form as energy. In effect what this chapter proposes is that the spiritual life, particularly of the ordained person, needs to adopt the spirit of the anagogical approach to the personal memory, just as we need to have that same spirit in the exploration of the Scriptures and the meaning of sacraments.

A Model of the Self

Julian of Norwich wrote, "We can never come to the full knowledge of God until we first clearly know our own soul."[1] There is a contemporary feeling to this statement, but it also has its particular historical background. This fourteenth-century spiritual guide was apparently thinking of exemplarism. This was that an analogue of the Triune Godhead is to be found within each person in the triune relationship between memory, intellect or understanding, and will. In this way, Julian probably thought, we come face-to-face with the mystery of the Trinity. Whether or not we find exemplarism helpful, however, the advice to look carefully within ourselves is well taken.

Some model of the self other than the relationship between memory, will, and understanding needs to be provided, however. But it is important to state from the outset that a model is no better than its heuristic value. It is a means for a greater understanding and is to be judged by capacity to serve within the larger truth. Every age must seek its own way to construct these models as guides to that universal need to know and experience ourselves as we really are that we might know God.

The human sciences seek a better understanding of the self. All kinds of models have been advanced. Among these prototypes, to name only a few of the better known, are the theories of psychoanalysis, sociobiology, behaviorism, structural functionalism, and humanistic psychology. The reaction of theologians has tended to be either unqualified rejection born of ignorance or an unreflective adoption of one or the other of them born of bad theology. In both instances the heuristic nature of a model was forgotten.

In my judgment the most helpful model of the self from the human sciences is that developed in dialogue with the work of C. G. Jung, but I would like to qualify my assertion in at least three ways. First, the insights of Jung assist in the area of the particular concern I have concerning the self: its spiritual maturation. I do not believe he is as helpful in other areas of theology, such as in liberation theology. Second, the appeal of Jung's pilgrimage is to my own history. I think that he probably does not speak as immediately to people younger than forty or to those who would find his subtle, gradual, and thoughtful entree into the psyche insufficiently aggressive. Jung is not for everyone. Third, doctrinaire Jungians are as a rule more a hindrance than a help in appropriating the model for the purposes of spiritual theology. When Jung's teaching is made into a system its claims become ultimate, rather than penultimate, and God's surprise is disallowed.

Jung understood himself as a scientist. He did not consider himself a theologian. Whereas he strayed more than once into the theologian's realm (e.g., in *Answer to Job*), he made no attempt to find a common theoretical base with theology. In fact, this is lacking in all the psychologies, which may be one important reason why theologians either reject psychology out of hand or swallow it whole, without spitting out the bones. There is great difficulty in differentiating the respective competencies of psychology and theology and of relating them into a meaningful whole. An immediate problem is a shared vocabulary, as, for example, the word "self."

It is particularly in response to Jung that a number of theologians and religious writers have been attempting to build this common theoretical base, while some clinicians in the world of spiritual direction have been using Jung's insights in developing the prayer life. Those at the Thomas Merton Center in Quebec are a somewhat controversial example of the latter, as are those at the Guild for Psychological Studies in California. Two Episcopal priests, John Sanford and Morton Kelsey, are examples of the former. Kelsey in particular has attempted to make up through a flood of books and articles for what he sees as the failure of authors on prayer to take into account psychological theory. In this section I do not intend to duplicate his massive effort but merely call the attention of the reader to some fundamental aspects of Jung's model which are helpful for understanding the relationship of the unconscious to prayer.

Jung maintained that the experience of the mystery of being has natural roots. What this means, as interpreted by theology, is that the energy of God as it infuses the person is spontaneously clothed in an incarnate form. This embodiment of the divine power goes on at all levels of our objectification of experience—from primal urge to conceptualization. Humankind is by nature open to the experience of God and at a primordial level of being we respond to that presence even if at an intellectual level we reject the possibility of God. "Whether called or not called," Jung was fond of quoting from Erasmus, and as I have already said, "God is there." To put it another way, we pray unconsciously, without ever being aware of it, inasmuch as prayer is the expressed relationship between God and humanity.

Prayer is a more immediate possibility at the deeper levels of the self. At those points the memory is less contaminated with the conventions of secularism or of the expectations of a domesticated deity. The surface memory quickly reduces God to a caricature readily rejected or to the less risky categories of civil religion.

When I was a university chaplain there were both an annual horse show and a rodeo at the institution I served. As the father of four young children, for whom both events were occasions of great excitement, I "bought" a ring seat box for us all by taking my turn offering the opening prayer on a given evening. What a wonderful opportunity this moment presented for a meditation upon the unconscious reasons for our fascination with riding sleek horses and with wrestling raging bulls. I might have begun with a text from God's speech to Job out of the whirlwind.

> *"Behold, Behemoth,*
> *which I made as I made you;*
> *he eats grass like an ox.*
> *Behold, his strength in his loins,*
> *and his power in the muscles of*
> *his belly . . .*
> *Can you draw out Leviathan*
> *with a fishhook,*
> *or press down his tongue with a*
> *cord?"*
> (Job 40:15–16, 41:1 rsv)

The Behemoth is more than a hippopotamus and the Leviathan more than a crocodile—probably their original animal identifications—they are symbols of the mystery of evil within us. William Blake (1757–1827) made much of both of them in this vein in his illustrations for *The Marriage of Heaven and Hell*. The mastery of beasts has always been an image of the spiritual struggle in the Judeo-Christian tradition.

But no one at a horse show, at a rodeo, or at Sunday service for that matter is interested in prayer that plumbs the depths of our passion. We feel much better with entertainment that safely titillates, any rush of primeval passion having been previously tamed by the opening prayer reminding us that we are God-fearing people. There is something in gladiatorial combat more authentic, if barbaric, to the dark side of the self than a sporting event cosmetized by the local pastor.

But in so cosmetizing we are the losers. If we are to live in intimate prayer with God we have to pass by way of the Behemoth and the Leviathan that is inside every one of us. This was not clearly recognized by the sample surveyed for this study. In answer to the statement, "One must risk evil if he is to know the meaning of the good," six agreed, four were undecided, one disagreed, and four strongly disagreed. One wonders what the understanding of the cross is in those who disagreed. In discerning the relationship between prayer and the unconscious we learn that the way to wholeness always lies through evil, that is, by way of the cross.

Edward Edinger, an analytical psychologist writing on religion and the unconscious, says, "Modern man's most urgent need is to discover the reality and value of the inner subjective world of the psyche, to discover the symbolic life."[2] Discovering the psyche or the self is to discover the symbolic life. It is symbols that invade our consciousness and invite us into a deeper understanding of the self in all its ambiguity.

The symbol that most readily leads us within ourselves is the feminine. In those who reject a movement into the consciousness and its implications for prayer, we would expect resistance to the feminine symbol and all that the feminine evokes in the spiritual life within them. It is suggestive that of the four clergy who strongly rejected the notion that if one is to know the good he must risk evil, the canonic outlook—a viewpoint that shapes its experience in terms of duty and law—was dominant in three and second only to the empirical outlook in the fourth. All four make decisions, according to the Meyers-Briggs, on the basis of analysis rather than feeling. In those first three there was a strong preference for structure. The same three were more masculine than feminine on the Bem Sex Role Inventory. The fourth was the exception that "tests" my hypothesis. He preferred spontaneity to structure and was more feminine than masculine by a little on the BSRI.

If we contrast the six persons who agreed that one must risk evil to know the good with the sample above, certain differences can be noted. With one exception, none of the six had a predominantly canonic worldview. The one who did had an equally predominant empiric outlook. Four had a higher empirical score than anything else, which means they tend to view the world as they think it is. One had a stronger charismatic viewpoint, which means he saw the world as evidence of God's providential hand. On the Myers-Briggs five of them were intuitive, feeling persons. The sixth was an intuitive, thinking person. The question of the preference for structure versus spontaneity was evenly divided: There was no discernable difference on the BSRI.

In Jungian theory the feminine encourages intuition and feeling. The masculine resists the seductions of the unconscious by analysis, structure, and an appeal to law. I think there is little doubt that in our sample we discover this dynamic at work. It suggests that an unwillingness to become aware of the feminine in the male inhibits the enrichment of the life of prayer by the symbols of the deep memory. This would also tend to keep the appreciation of Scripture and the sacraments at a conceptual level.

Why do some resist the call of their feminine? The probability lies in a fact already mentioned. When the feminine stirs within us and leads us deeper into ourselves it awakens us to our dark side. We must of necessity confront the evil that is part of each of us and threatens to destroy us. Gregory of Nyssa speaks in his own way to this point: "The assault of the Adversary accompanies the ascent of virtue and seeks out corresponding opportunities to subvert toward evil, as the people improve in the godly life."[3] Teresa of Avila refers to the same thing when she writes, "There are few dwelling places in this castle [of the inner self] in which the devils do not wage battle."[4]

The point is that spiritual growth requires that we do battle, not that we pretend the enemy is not there. The journey into the wilderness by the desert fathers in the early church to fight the demons and to discover the angels is an analogue of our own inner journey into the unconscious. Perhaps the greatest fault of persons who claim an immediate, intimate relationship with Jesus, based upon an experience of consolation, is their blindness to the evil that persists within each of us. This evil, hidden beneath a pseudo-goodness, only continues to eat away at us unless acknowledged as our own and confronted in the name of Christ.

For it is the image of Christ within the self to which the feminine within, the inner *theotokos* ("God-bearer") would lead us. The corporate image of the feminine in the church is of course the Mother of our Lord. The appeal of Mary to the Christian is that she gives theological substance to that feminine that is within us and becomes the prototype of every woman who evokes within man his spiritual self. She (the spiritual feminine) gives birth within his spirit to the Christ. The threat of Mary is that once freed from a cloying sentimentality she confronts the presumption of the inflated male. We resist her for the same reason we resist our inner feminine: both challenge our illusions of control.

For Mary, the church's collective feminine, evokes in us not just a warm recollection of the womb, but a premonition of the tomb as well. The similar resonance of womb and tomb is not merely accidental. She is also not only a recollection of the nurturing mother, but of the fear of consuming passion. The relationship of fecundity to death lies buried within the memory of each of us. She who would lead us to

Christ would bring us through the darkness of the inner self to him who is the divine made incarnate that we might be whole.

A striking response, if not surprising, was the widespread affirmation of the image of the Blessed Virgin in the piety of the research sample. The role of Mary as *theotokos* was generally valued. If there were any negative comments, they came from an Episcopalian and a Roman Catholic. One Lutheran pastor observed, "I think it [the image of the Blessed Virgin] needs to be more developed, particularly for Lutherans. I think I've even had what I think was a vision of her in a dream." He then went on to tell of an experience of healing in which he was instrumental involving the use of water from the spring at Lourdes.

What I have said about the feminine as she who leads the person within the self to the Christ relates to men. In women this is the function of the masculine principle, what Jung called the *animus*. One of the ordained women in this study, who was familiar with the terminology of analytical psychology, described the masculine in her as a shaman who points the way within. "The animus mediates God/spiritual experiences," she said,

> and provides a groundedness which enables me to ask the questions and search for meaning in an unflinching way. Further, I am able to step back and take an objective look at the meaning of experience and question former "mind-sets." My animus is an inner companion who invests/strengthens me with those attributes we consider masculine, for example, objectivity, indomitable spirit, initiative, and receptivity to new ideas and concerns.

I recall a dream told to me by an ordained woman who was married. Her husband is a well-integrated, strong person, who manages things well and inspires confidence. Her dream was of walking through a forest with her husband. They came to the mouth of a cave and she stepped into that chthonic world, but her husband stood outside. Within, another male figure, whom she recognized as a friend who is a priest, took her hand and together they explored the cave. The friend embodied in her dream that spiritual *animus*, which her husband could not be to her. It is the spiritual *animus*, the shaman, that accompanies the woman on her inner journey, just as every male needs his *theotokos*. Perhaps John of the Cross embodied this for Teresa of Avila.

Paul wrote the church in Rome, "Let your minds be remade and your whole nature thus transformed"(Rom. 12:2). It is clear that he understood this to happen when we are "in Christ," which, in effect, means when the historical Jesus, who is in fact the Christ, is in us as the governing image of our deep memory. As the Christian makes the inner journey in the company of the Scriptures and the sacraments, he or she does in fact find at the apogee of the journey him who is the primal sacrament of God. Jung's point that Christ is the archetype of the whole self carries in part this same meaning.

In fact, the non-Christian who makes the inner journey finds at the apogee of the quest this same figure, but he or she does not know his name. The Christian claim is that the search for the image of the whole person, the *Urmensch* or primordial human, is fulfilled in Christ. This is at least suggested in the relationship between the son of man in Daniel 7:13—specifically so named only in the Greek version of the Old Testament—and references in the New Testament to Jesus as the son of man. It may be true that Daniel only speaks of the angel of the Jewish people in referring to the son of man. It was a common notion in the second century b.c. that every nation had such an angel. But it makes sense that there was a psychological connection between this idea and that image that prevails in the mythology of most peoples of the primordial human, who is the divine pattern for us all.

One version of the fulfillment of the search for the primordial human is in Logos Christology. When the New Testament speaks of Jesus as the Logos what is being said is that the incomprehensible abyss, which we call God the Father, has the capacity to make himself known in our corporate and individual histories. In the Logos both God is truly revealed and true man perfectly represented. We plumb the depths of the Christian self and come into the presence of the sacrament of that meeting between our humanity and God: the Logos, he who is embodied in the historical Jesus of Nazareth. This Christ is the nexus of our prayer with God, which is why Christians pray in his name.

Bonaventure, in what may be an excess of Franciscan piety, cites the Song of Songs as he describes Christ as the inner sacrament of God.

With Christ I am nailed to the cross . . .
An affection and feeling of this kind
is merited to be experienced in a vital way only by one
who, not unmindful of the Lord's passion nor ungrateful,
contemplates

the labor, suffering and love
of Jesus crucified,
with such vividness of memory, such sharpness of intellect
and such charity of will
that he can truly say with the bride:
A bundle of myrrh is my beloved to me;
he will linger
between my breasts.[5]

The appeal to memory, intellect, and will is a reference to the inner journey. There in our inmost heart, which lies between the breasts, we find the image of Jesus crucified, the archetype of the whole person.

Knowing the Unknown Knowing

A priest spoke of the turning points in his life in this manner: "I gradually became aware over a period of time that I've already known I should do something for quite a long time . . . You've been heading for this for a long time. This time you recognize it." This sense of coming to know something he had already known describes the experience of having made a decision at one level of one's mind, only later to consciously acknowledge it.

The same priest, who was raised in a strongly evangelical background, spoke of his adolescent spiritual struggle. All his youth he had heard it said that one must make a "fresh start." But life for him could not be an unending succession of fresh starts. "I had to play into something that would be a process of growth." This process of growth is a coming to know what we already know at that point where the horizon of the self impinges upon the infinite presence of God. This border country of the interior self is what the author of *The Cloud of Unknowing* calls "a naked intention directed to God and himself alone," or a "blind outreaching of love."[6] Shrouded in the darkness of unknowing God illumines the mind with a knowing of which we do not yet know.

Another pastor who was converted from unbelief to an evangelical tradition spoke of the same experience in this way:

It's kind of like a peak experience with growth up to and growth out of. The Lord was working very strongly and very uniquely at the time, I think, when I committed my life to Christ: laying the head foundation to understand who Christ is. The expansion of consciousness [at the time of commitment] God did for me. The other stuff was a learning process, sorting things out in my head.

This pastor does not speak of the unknown knowing that had gone on, yet by implication it is there: "growth up to" the experience of commitment, followed by the "growth out of," which is a "sorting out" of the "head foundation."

Knowing the unknown is the surfacing of unconscious prayer. Generally we live our life at the predictable level of the surface memory and those interactions dedicated by social custom that we have learned from birth. This is as true of the ordained person as of anyone else. Even in these times of role confusion, the average pastor acquires by various means an understanding of what his superiors, colleagues, and people expect of him. Our age knows perhaps a greater degree of irritation at living out these expectations than earlier, more culturally homogeneous times; although we ought not to be too ingenuous about job satisfaction in generations past.

There come times, however, when the predictable pattern of clerical interaction fails to answer the questions we cannot avoid. We find ourselves challenged as pastors, tempted to behave or actually behaving in ways that radically contradict our own expectations of our self. More than one priest or pastor has said that the beginning of the exploration of the prayer of the unconscious began as he or she reflected upon a genital relationship with someone other than his or her spouse. The common sense routine of living works against the spiritual awakening of each of us. There needs to be that dramatic collapse of the taken-for-granted.

One person described his experience this way:

Sometimes the more I think, the more [turning points in my spiritual journey] I can find. I was thinking yesterday of two events that converged. One was the ministry in the hospital. I kept coming up with the question: What do I have that the doctors don't have? Second, there was a time of very strong personal temptation of the flesh. These two things at one point drove me to the Lord for guidance, on the one hand, and deliverance, on the other.

To be driven to the Lord, if we mean by that something other than looking in the Bible for "answers," is an experience of the prayer that continually goes on at the deeper levels of the self, beyond the expectations of the surface memory and its neat, predictable patterns of behavior. The pastor who described the convergence of these two events related an awakening to the meaning of his own life as an ordained person—a meaning that I daresay was there when God called him, perhaps while still in the womb.

An intentional life of prayer is not one, however, that waits until a secularly trained doctor confronts us in the hospital corridor or the thought lingers that an attractive parishioner might need more than just our words of wisdom. We need to work at knowing the unknown knowing, while recognizing that we can only approach this deep knowledge and can never grasp it in its entirety.

Meditation is the time-honored method for doing this. While even woolgathering is justified as meditating, I mean by meditation a disciplined method of exploring the deeper self in order to know the unknown known. Essentially it takes one of two paths. In Western Christianity we are strongly influenced by the Ignatian tradition, especially as it was developed by the French school of spirituality in the seventeenth century, with Francis de Sales, Jean-Jacques Olier, and others. This method, known as kataphatic, is a systematic free association upon biblical and other traditional images. In Eastern Christianity another tradition evolved, which continues to influence us in the West as well. Associated with figures such as Evagrius Ponticus and Gregory Palamas, it consists of a systematic effort to empty the mind and heart by the constant repetition of a simple prayer, such as the Jesus prayer ("Jesus, Christ, Son of God, Savior, have mercy on me"). This is known as apophatic prayer.

Perhaps a significant surprise in this study has been the indication that three-fourths of the persons interviewed tended toward a more apophatic spirituality (twelve out of sixteen). A key to this is the completion of the statement, "To approach God with empty hands and heart for me is . . ." The mean response to this approached "usually important" (3.4 on a scale of 1 to 5, n = 15). Only two persons reported that it was never important. Yet it is a question of how vigorously the ordained persons interviewed pursue the apophatic spirit since the "dark night of the soul," an inevitable consequence along the way, is only rarely to occasionally experienced (2.4 on a scale of 1 to

5, n = 15). Only two persons reported they never experienced the dark night, but only one reported he did frequently.

Psychologically speaking, meditation taps the prayer of the unconscious because it seeks to deautomate the socialized forms of thinking. If we keep in mind that we are taught by society to form reality automatically in a specific way, then we can understand that meditation serves to move beyond this learned pattern. In a secular society such as our own, where we are taught *not* to expect to experience God, it is particularly important that those who serve God cultivate an intentional model of prayer that breaks through the hard crust of the surface memory to the deeper self, which is relatively untouched by the collective representations of our environment. Secular society refers to this as "mysticism," which is an acceptable term despite the intended ridicule. The catch is that our world does not allow for the possibility that the mystical experience is true. Such experience is not something contemporary society can falsify; it is only the bias of the collective representation.

Meditation is a decision of the will resulting in an action to know the unknown known. The movement can be reversed. The unknown known can seek to become known by breaking into our consciousness. It does this in a variety of ways when our surface memory becomes inactive: a slip of the tongue, a thought that pops into our mind while driving down the interstate highway, or an insight that presents itself in the midst of a sermon or lecture we have given many times before. But the most common example is in dreams. It is interesting that a large majority of the clergy interviewed do not experience dreams as a form of prayer. Eleven out of sixteen responded that dreams rarely or never reveal God's purpose to them. Four did say, however, that occasionally or even frequently they do.

John Sanford, an Episcopal priest and analytical psychologist, has written a number of books teaching that dreams are "the forgotten language of God," to quote one of his titles. In one such book he told the story of a German *Luftwaffe* pilot in World War II, who underwent analysis for hysterical color blindness. In his dreams his adored brother, who was a member of the SS, appeared in a white uniform (SS uniforms were black) with a black face. His hated sister, who was a member of the underground in Germany, appeared with a face that was shining white. The pilot, who had been carefully trained in Hitler's Germany to think the Nazi cause righteous, was brought by

his dreams to discover that in fact he had been educated to make the
white black and the black white. Unable to bear the message of his
own inner self, he committed suicide.

This case illustrates the hypothesis that Sanford goes on to explain:

> Deep inside each organism is something that knows what
> that organism's true nature and life goal is. It is as though
> there is within each person an inner Center that knows what
> constitutes health. If our conscious personality becomes re-
> lated to the inner Center, the whole person may begin to
> emerge, though this may not bring either peace or social
> adaptation, but conflict and stress . . . The movement toward
> health may look more like a crucifixion than adaptation or
> peace of mind.[7]

The dreams become messages from a deeper level of the self than we
acknowledge in our fully conscious, socially shaped thinking. Often
the collective expectation blocks significant insights formed deep
within the self. Such insights can emerge on occasion from such great
depth that they reveal a level of unknown knowing that is at that horizon of the divine-human meeting.

A striking illustration of this dynamic was provided by one of the
clergy interviewed. He had indicated that his dreams frequently revealed God's purpose to him and I asked him to explain how he saw
this happening. "I write my sermons," he replied,

> many times at three in the morning when I wake up from a
> dream and put down what I've had [in my dream]. I go to
> bed on Friday night without worrying about whether there is
> a sermon. More often the real jelling of the sermon comes
> with Saturday afternoon or Sunday morning, and as often as
> not in a light sleep. I wake up and write it down in the mid-
> dle of the night.

This pastor noted that this was not his regular practice, but that it was
frequent enough for him to trust the process. In fact, he spoke of one
sermon in particular, which he considered to have been one of his
best, that was written just this way in the middle of the night.

Generally the language of dreams is oblique. If we are to hear their message we have to attend to them over a period of time, recording them and looking for patterns and recurring images. In other words, it is as important to be intentional about our dreams as it is our meditation. There is value in sharing our dream journal with someone skilled in understanding the language of dreams. The effect of a careful and regular acceptance of our dream life is to build into our consciousness a depth that reaches below the superficial interface between the world and ourselves, characterized by that mask with which we have learned to engage the expectations of ourselves *vis-à-vis* others. Both meditation and attention to our dreams provide a source of knowing that opens us to a new awareness of the God who speaks deep within us.

The Three D's

We have all been taught that still waters run deep. The gift of the awareness of unconscious prayer is an inner stillness that is expressed in the three D's of spiritual maturity: *detachment, discretion,* and *discernment.*

Detachment is not a popular notion in some theories of pastoral care. It seems to contradict the ideal of the empathetic relationship. Actually detachment is a necessary condition for effective empathy. *Detachment* means our freedom from being victimized by our own emotions and those to whom we minister. We can enter into a relationship with another person without contaminating it with unconscious garbage. To possess detachment is to know ourselves in depth so that we have a perspective upon our own reactions in relation to events and other people. The opposite of detachment is not compassion, it is seduction.

Detachment is like getting a clear signal on the television screen. So often we see God obscured by clutter. Occasionally in the interviews clergy would say they had rejected traditional expressions of piety because the people whom they witnessed as examples of such piety did not live heroic Christian lives. They were obsessed with their own needs, they were blind to human suffering, and they reacted rather than acted. Their vision of God was full of clutter. Despite their aspirations for a holy life, they lacked detachment.

They also lacked *discretion*, a term that comes from Richard of St. Victor. Discretion is the product of reason. It is interesting that in Richard's extended allegory, *The Twelve Patriarchs*, Joseph the dreamer stands for discretion and is born of Rachel, who is reason. Because he

can interpret dreams he possesses discretion. Richard means by discretion an Aristotelian moderation or golden mean: "nothing too
much." The discreet person in this sense tempers the excess of virtue
that leads to pride and self-righteousness. Discretion is the result of
knowing ourselves and a precondition to knowing God. "The soul
that has not been practiced over a long time," says Richard, "and educated fully in knowledge of self is not raised up to the knowledge of
God."[8] If we know ourselves we will possess humility which is the
proper soil—if the reader will pardon the obscure play on words—for
the word of God.

A priest of my acquaintance is fond of describing people who
"love Jesus lots." He is mocking a peculiar insensitivity of enthusiasm,
which does not have the discretion to recognize the subtlety of an authentic experience of prayer.

A favorite biblical story of mine is Elijah's flight into the wilderness just ahead of Jezebel's assassins. First he was under a broom
bush, then on Mount Horeb, and finally at the mouth of a cave. Each
place God asked Elijah the same inane question, "Why are you here,
Elijah?" Of course, it was God's angel that led him on and Elijah expected God to tell him why he was there. But there was no answer
from the wind, the earthquake, or the fire. Finally, Elijah heard God in
a "low murmuring sound," but he still asked the same question, "Why
are you here, Elijah?" (1 Kings 19:1–14).

Elijah had discretion. Nothing seemed to go right. He wanted to
die. But he could still listen. Spiritual instruction can be very costly.
This is different indeed from the washed-in-the-blood enthusiast, ex-
uding the confidence of a used car salesman. The persistent questioning of our motives, driving us to an ever deeper self-knowledge, misses
him. The subtle inquiry that leads to a knowledge of God's will therefore eludes his grasp.

As discretion builds on detachment, so discernment follows from
them both. *Discernment* is the ability to intuit God's will by casting the
particular question of what the Christian should do in a given situation before the judgment of the deeper self. Moralism is a sure sign of
an obdurate conscience and a heart closed to God. The alternative is
the willingness to risk decisions whose surety is enigmatic at best. We
have to trust to the intimations of the self as it ponders the divine purpose at the edge of our knowing.

The ability to discern the will of God requires acuity, attention,
and apperception. One must be sensitive to the slightest hint, look at

it closely, and reflect with an ear to the inner hunch. This certainly requires an openness in prayer to the angels of the unconscious and the courage to judge in response to a word whispered in the dark of night.

Conclusion

Teresa of Avila in describing the interior castle speaks of the first rooms as those of self-knowledge. But she makes self-knowledge not simply the prerequisite for knowing God, and turns the usual statement on its head. "Let's strive to make more progress in self-knowledge," she says; but surprisingly she adds, "for in my opinion we shall never know ourselves if we don't strive to know God."[9] This apparent paradox—we must seek to know ourselves in order that we might know God so that we might know ourselves—arises from Teresa's conviction that all the rooms of the castle of the soul face inward to the royal chamber of the King, from whence they receive their light.

The prayer of the unconscious is a pilgrimage through the rooms of the soul, but the source of their light is God who lies beyond our deepest memory and seeks to make himself known in every apartment of our being.

9. A Parish Piety

EVERY Christian shares in liturgical prayer, and every person prays out of the unconscious. But what is peculiar to the priest or pastor is the relationship between that person as a spiritual being and his or her responsibility to a congregation. For whatever our particular theology of ordination may be, there is a dynamic underlying all explanations that places a unique burden and gives a special opportunity to those who serve a parish as pastor. There is very little in the literature of the Christian spiritual masters that is specifically directed to the parish priest or pastor.

It would appear that those with special gifts in prayer were either lay persons or clerics who lived out their lives as hermits or as members of religious communities, in which case they had the leisure to pray, to think, and to write. It is doubtful whether before the seventeenth century many active parish clergy had the ability to write, not to mention the time or inclination, although there are exceptions to this historical silence from the parish. George Herbert was a country parson; and, indeed, some of his poems are reflections upon the church building. Johann Arndt, the Lutheran mystic beloved by the Pietists, is another, although his writings say little about the relationship between parish and prayer.

Part of what lies behind the silence is the understanding of the task of the parish pastor. It was thought to be that of an ambassador of Christ, and there was no consideration given to how the congregation fed the ordained person. This was true even in the Middle Ages, when the functions of ministry were more widely shared than they have been in the last four hundred years. The idea of role and a supportive community is unique to the twentieth century, as is the notion that the pastor's own frailty is an instrument of effective ministry (as in the "wounded healer"). The first book to open for me the possibility of a fertile relationship between the routine of parish ministry and the spiritual life was by Leo Trese, entitled *Vessel of Clay*. Trese, who was a Roman Catholic priest, shared the wanderings of his mind that lay behind his appearance in the role of the proper priest. As a seminarian I found this very liberating. It also offered the possibility that there might be some enriching connection between what I as a parish priest did and how I might pray.

The question that arises at this point is whether or not there is a parish piety, distinct from an eremitical, monastic, or lay piety? I think in fact I there is, but it is difficult to state and answers are even less frequently attempted. Current ministry studies are of almost no help here. The sterility of the professional model of ministry, which has dominated American pastoral care for half a century, makes the problem almost unsurmountable. If prayer ever gets mentioned in this model, which is rarely, it is only in terms of pietism.

Yet the attempt needs to be made to begin an understanding of parish piety. One person I interviewed complained that theologians—he tactfully did not say "*you* theologians"—need to reflect on the reality of parish life. Certainly one place to start would be in spiritual theology.

Probity, Gravity, and Priority

One of the greatest difficulties the contemporary priest or pastor experiences is spiritual discipline. I mean by this much more than setting aside specific times for prayer. Rather it is a question of self-knowledge. Can we understand ourselves in terms of our inner intentions, reaching into the deep memory, and maintain the authenticity of the internal structure of self in relation to the parish? As I see it, this is the crucial issue of vocation. The call is an awareness emerging from within oneself. Can its authenticity be maintained in the face of parish life? The ongoing, daily resolution of this issue requires insight fed from our deep inner life. There is no way that the spirituality of the ordained person can be realized short of being responsible for himself or herself as a hearer of the Word.

A number of recent studies of the clergy—a good example is John Harris' *Stress, Power, and Ministry*[1]—do an excellent job of describing the dilemma of the pastor and some action pastors might take with respect to their own vocation. But what Harris and others so clearly demonstrate needs to be extended to its implications for spiritual theology. The life of prayer depends upon an awareness of ourselves in relation to the pressures of being a parish pastor and the support and guidance that enables us to claim and reclaim our vocation.

Often what gets said is that the pastor's job depends upon his or her meeting the expectations of the congregation or that promotion comes to only those who prostitute their own spiritual integrity. Clergy seminars are filled with accounts of situations where efforts to pattern the Sunday worship in accordance with the best in theological and historical knowledge are met with anger and threats by the people. There is a current rash of clergy terminations that from all appearances have resulted from the pastor's desire to reach outside the "old guard" to those who are looking for institutional support for an authentic religious experience.

It is just as important, however, to see the point of view of the laity. In a series of conferences held for the laity while engaged in the research for this book, we asked what helps and what hinders the effectiveness of a parish. It was clear from the replies that the priest or pastor is almost always the key, and the prevailing answer was that it depends on her or his willingness to let others minister. Specific clergy who received praise were ones of whom they said: "He trusts us," "She is not threatened by new ideas," or "If we come up with an idea, he encourages us to try it." The power of the ordained person to enable the ministry of the laity is remarkable. Pastors who frustrated and angered the laity were those who maintained control by being resistant and opaque. Of course, the laity inclined to come to such conferences are those who want things to happen in the parish.

A spirituality rooted in a parish has no chance as long as there is a we/they split between the ordained leadership and the people. The common realization that some pastors look upon the people as the enemy and that some laity consider the pastor a scandal cannot do anything but choke that openness to God that is the presupposition of the life of prayer. A resolution between expectations must occur as the result of a mutual honesty or probity.

This resolution does not come through a *wholesale, unreflective* incorporation of secular organizational development theory. A good illustration of the debate over the ordained ministry as profession or vocation can be drawn from the implications of such theory. For example, the use of a contract as a means of determining the terms of employment—principally defining what the priest or pastor will *not* do—is found by many church people to be negative and offensive. The expectations of evaluation based upon performance goals has resulted in either a gross reduction of the meaning of ministry—how does one evaluate a symbol and symbol-bearer?—or proven to be an exercise in futility.

But there is an absolute need for building a basic, explicit direction for the work of the pastor, in which the ordained person and the parish leadership share. Some of the illusions of the pastor's total availability and omniscience need to be dispelled. Some clergy have found that if in such a covenant with their parish they are open about the time spent in prayer, the need to be with their family or friends, and the desire for provisions for continuing education, they find a surprising gratitude on the part of those they serve to know that their pastor is doing these things.

In our time, late vocations are more common and more men and women leave for seminary after living ten or twenty years as adults in a parish. As they go, their congregations feel a certain pride and invest definite expectations in them. Yet sometimes these lay people become angry when these persons return to the parish different from the way they were when they left; they seem no longer effective. It is possible that a seminary education can render its graduates ineffective, but far more likely it demonstrates that the pastor and his or her people will inevitably see things with different perspectives. One of those persons interviewed suggested that theological jargon was the chief sin of the clergy. Without doubt we all have our particular point of view, but I am inclined to think that a far greater sin is when parish clergy try to forget their seminary education in order to please those they serve. Inevitably, this creates a tension within the pastor because he or she intentionally does not tap his or her own knowledge. What you have is a person avoiding his or her best insights.

It is apparent, however, that the clergy not only have a different outlook from the laity's, but that this is necessary. It comes with the role of the prophet, which is indissolubly linked to the pastoral function. The absence of prophetic insight makes for a very poor pastor. All of this points to the need for ordained persons to accept their "difference" and not pretend that a solution to differing expectations and the loneliness that accompanies them is to conform themselves to what others expect. The beginning of an answer to what one does with this difference is that the pastor or priest needs to claim his or her own intention as shaped by what he or she hears as God's call. There is no solution in terms of spiritual theology to the problems of the parish clergy that can avoid the need for an articulate in-depth self-knowledge.

The concluding chapter is concerned with ways of approaching this self-knowledge, but here it should be said that, first, the quest never ends and, second, we are never free of the threat of being captured by the negative self. I knew of a priest well educated in the human sciences, regarded as gifted, who from time to time would write an irrational, self-destructive outburst. Despite personal therapy, he never acquired the detachment, discretion, and discernment to understand what he was doing. The pursuit of self-knowledge is for a lifetime and we are never secure from our own darkness.

Athanasius (c.296–373) in *The Life of Antony*, an account that had great influence on the church of his day, offers timeless illustrations of this struggle. Athanasius describes in his hagiography a series of confrontations between Antony and the devil. In the first real struggle, having failed to defeat Antony in his initial sallies, the devil assumes a visage in Antony's mind and sexually tempts him. Antony resists and by God's power wins a victory. "But," says Athanasius,

> Antony did not then become careless or arrogant, as though the devil were conquered, nor did the enemy, like someone who had failed, cease from setting traps. For once again he was prowling around like a lion seeking some opportunity for attack.[2]

There is a power in the direct simplicity of this story. One wonders what Athanasius was experiencing that led him to record it in his writing, but it may well have been the kind of experience that might have parallels today.

The spiritual discipline that constitutes the core of self-knowledge within the priest or pastor comes to be the center from which his or her life within the parish is shaped. Perhaps it is important to remind ourselves that, when explored, this internal structure of meaning acquires a coherency and direction that open out on the mystery of the divine presence. As we identify the mystagogue within ourselves, so are we better able to be the mystagogue to the people whom God has called us to serve.

The internal energy flows naturally outward from us into the life of the parish. Decisions are related to the intention that is formed within ourselves and consequently focused upon the parish life. The hoped-for effect is to enable us to make judgments of *probity, gravity,* and *priority*. To make these judgments is to answer these questions: What shall I *not* do? What shall I do? What shall I do first?

I have a friend who grew up in the marshlands of southern Louisiana. He is a good man with whom to walk those swamps, because he can smell a snake before anyone sees it. It is an acquired skill. Hollow men and women do not even know evil when they see it, much less smell it. They have shunned the discipline to acquire the skill.

Not infrequently clergy are caught up in the evil that threatens every congregation because they have no ability to discern what in fact is happening. Illustrations abound: adultery, greed, cowardice, and omnipotence. But the sin to which ordained persons particularly given is envy. We are told that it is for envy that Christ was betrayed (Matt. 27:18). James attributes the quarrels among his readers to envy (James 4:1–8); and Clement of Rome in his letter to the Corinthians tells the church there that their greatest problem is envy. William Law (1686–1761) said that envy is "acknowledged by all people to be the most ungenerous, base, and wicked passion that can enter into the heart of man."[3] Envy is no stranger to the clergy today. One experienced spiritual director suggested to me that it above everything else keeps the clergy from helping their people grow spiritually. Envy prevails within parish life, and too often the pastor becomes sucked up into it and set at odds with laity and clergy alike.

There is an old saying in the practice of medicine: first do no harm. It applies to the practice of ministry as well. The discipline of the spirit begins by making us sensitive to what *not* to do by enabling us to know the destructive motivation that lies within ourselves. This is *probity*. We all fail, but if, for example, we are immune to the rank odor of envy, we blame the failure on others and we pass that moment of grace untouched.

As one comes to know the large questions within himself or herself and ceases to live in terms of the debris floating on the surface of the mind, then the ability is present to make judgments of the *gravity* of the issues that surround us. The priests and pastors interviewed in this study as a whole did not share that often-heard complaint of clergy that they spend their time on trivia or that they are incurably busy doing unimportant things. I assume this is because they had come to some conclusion as to what it is that is worth doing. It takes a living, growing sense of the integrity of our vocation to make that judgment in the face of the pressures of parish life.

A great deal of the frustration reported by priests and pastors in the parish is related to the feeling, first, that what they do is in reaction to demands placed upon them rather than chosen as a result of their intention for their ministry; and, second, that what they do as a result of reacting is often trivial, if not menial. There is among those who lay their expectations upon the clergy no compelling vision of the function of the priest or pastor. I am more than doubtful that we can ever abolish a certain amount of reactive ministry. The goal is to seek a balance between it and a proactive ministry, where what the pastor does is a result of certain objectives that person holds for his or her ministry.

The character of life that can enable us to accomplish a reasonably happy compromise and to become less outer-directed and more inner-directed is one in which we are open to the Spirit. A gentle, yet persistent, pursuit of prayer can help us claim our vocation. From this point the decisions of what to do have an inner integrity. Athanasius again speaks of Antony, when he came out of a hermitage of twenty years, in words characteristic of his times but with value to this late twentieth century:

> The state of his [Antony's] soul was one of purity, for it was not constricted by grief, nor relaxed by pleasure, nor affected by either laughter or dejection. Moreover, when he saw the crowd, he was not annoyed any more than he was elated at being embraced by so many people. He maintained utter equilibrium, like one guided by reason and steadfast in that which accords with nature.[4]

We may not be comfortable with the spirit of *apatheia* that lies behind the words of Athanasius, but the sense of being our own person in relation to God is as valid now as it was then.

Because the parish ministry requires compromise, an unwillingness to do this is more a sign of spiritual pride than of spiritual depth. The issue is one of priorities. We have to determine where we must follow our own vision for the sake of the Gospel and where we need to heed someone else for the same reason. The Gospel we know in prayer.

I once served a small congregation on the shore of Lake Michigan. There is no community from which I have been more enriched. We had built a small, interesting building on a large piece of property looking out over the town and the lake beyond. In the summer wildflowers grew up around the church to a height of about three feet; one was a lovely blue flower. One Sunday I came into the church to find two men of the parish standing in front of the plate glass window across the east end. They immediately drew me into the conversation. One was saying that the tall weeds attracted rats and if we did not mow the field before next Sunday he was withdrawing his pledge. The other man, whose daughter was to be married there the following Saturday, replied that if we did mow it he was withdrawing his pledge. Each one gave about a fifth of the budget. What did I think? The only answer I could give consistent with my priorities for that parish was to say, "Men, you have a problem!"

I had an opinion, of course; I liked the grass and flowers waving in the breeze. But I saw myself according to my vocation in that parish as the sacramental person (i.e., the symbol-bearer and the symbol) and to take sides would have compromised that function. The decision was theirs. The field was mowed within twenty-five feet of the building, incidentally, and the rest left wild.

It is the spiritual life of the ordained person that is the source of meeting the issues of probity, gravity, and priority within the parish.

Events of Enrichment

But it is clear that the parish also provides those occasions in which our awareness of God's presence is broken open. One pastor spoke to me of his belief that academic or systematic theology did little for him as one who ministered to a congregation. His life was enriched in a different way: "My life is mostly out there where these people are and live," he said.

> Then I have to have something to stand on myself as I relate with them. The questions that I have to raise are not the questions that some theologians deal with. For example, we had four deaths in our parish last week. One of the members who died was a spinster schoolteacher who lived sixty-eight years before she died of cancer. She came back to us three years ago. I came to know and appreciate her.
>
> As it was discovered she had this cancer I would visit quite often and find her in all conditions. She would raise many questions. "Why do I have cancer? I always took care of my body, watched what I ate. I only smoked for a year and a

half and I got plenty of rest. Why do I have cancer?" Then we would go into other things of God and of life.

The questions that I would have would not be those that she would raise as such, but I would have to wrestle with who is this person in God's life and her life. How do I treat her as a person? From time to time I would ask the good old pastoral questions: Are you at peace with God? You seem to me to be at peace. Are you that much at peace? Always she would say, "Yes." She is witnessing to me the life of a faithful child of God. That to me is theology.

Then this pastor went on to tell me what she told him of her understanding of herself as a person. It was that she was like an iceberg. Only a very small part of her was known to anyone including herself. The rest was shrouded in mystery; but it was the mystery that held her up. This pastor was made aware in a very profound way of the inner mystery of his own self as he reflected upon the words of his dying parishioner, and what he found "to stand on" was her gift to him of faith.

Another priest whose parish is generally made up of young, energetic, and upwardly mobile people, described a woman who at thirty died in her sleep beside her husband. It was a very rare cardiac failure. The trauma was immense in that congregation, where the general expectation of the membership from all appearances was of immortality. I asked how this affected his spiritual growth. He reflected on that experience and others in that place (in seven years of ministry and nine funerals he has not had a single lingering death and no one has been over fifty), in the light of his earlier feelings.

I had great fears of it [death]. It is a great mystery. It was a fearful mystery for me—tremendously fearful, and I found that as I was doing my clinical experience [in seminary] I felt very much motivated—it was very much an experience of the holy in the *mysterium tremendum*. I was fascinated yet frightened and scared—just terrified of it. I wanted to be closer, but I couldn't be.

I am working very much with hospice now. I have seen that really change the direction of how I feel and think. It has gone from significant fear to the acceptance of the reality of death as a part of life, seeing it as giving meaning to life. It gives definition, it sets time limits. It is not just something I have to hide from. I don't agree anymore with the image of death as being the ugly, unwanted stranger, but rather as a very necessary aspect of this humanity I share.

More than one clergy person has spoken of a personal tragedy within the parish as a pivotal occasion for spiritual growth. One such pastor came to a parish only to have his three-year-old son die of leukemia very shortly after arriving. This tragedy, as he said,

> led me to start looking. I learned a lot of things at seminary, I think, on an intellectual level about the resurrection and the [future?] life. I don't think it was too much a part of me. So I started a journey here. That led me into a deeper walk through meditation and the prayer life.

He then described an occasion when shortly after his son's death he was blessing a child at the altar. The child reported that he felt an energy come into him, which both frightened and perplexed this pastor. He went on to say:

> I have since come to believe that God was telling me I had the gift of healing; to pray for the sick and things would happen. I have since done that and things do happen when I really feel I am prompted by the Lord. My walk has been right here in this congregation.

All three of these illustrations are from the experience of death. This should not surprise us. The fundamental metaphor of the Christian story is that as we die with Christ we are raised with him. Death is the condition of life. We discover our life in our identification with death, particularly as it is experienced collaboratively. Perhaps the principal pastoral paradigm for the Christian life is the ministry to the dying, because we are all dying. This is the ultimate truth about us, and the truth is that ours is a ministry of ultimates.

The power of death to awaken us to the presence of God speaking to us is particularly urgent in our times. We live in an age that values control. Theologians like to be able to explain things so there are no questions, young executives want to be on top of their work, and new pastors wish to appear to their people to have their lives together.

Death comes and renders these assumptions of control a shambles. Then in our chaos and our dependency we cry to God. Then and perhaps only then we can hear.

In many ways the capacity for such experiences as these to achieve clarity and focus is found in the life of the community. This is particularly true in the congregation's ritual. The illustration of the iceberg became a part of the funeral homily for the spinster schoolteacher. Without question the congregation of people-on-the-way-up dealt with the shock of death's visit to one of their number in the context of the requiem Eucharist, in which we are nourished by the death of Christ at age thirty-three. It was at the altar, broken by the death of his son, that the pastor first sensed the call to the healing ministry.

For myself there will always be deeply embedded in my memory the image of Kiera. When she was three she came with her parents and little brother to seminary, so that her father might study for the priesthood. She was a delightful little girl, very bright and articulate. She knew as did many of us that she was not well and would never get well. I remember vividly the Maundy Thursday Eucharist, when the Dean washes the feet of members of the seminary community, that she sat on her father's lap and I washed her five-year-old feet. She laughed at the feel of the water and the towel. As I knelt there it was as if I bowed before an all too young Sister Death—as Francis of Assisi was wont to call her—a blithe spirit, leading us into a better world. Kiera died the next August in her mother's arms. Her last words were, "I feel like I'm flying." I committed her ashes to that common earth from which we all come and to which we all shall return; but I have faith that with her we shall fly to the One.

The experience of a physical death with the parish is not the only occasion for spiritual growth noted by those interviewed. Any event that breaks open the surface self and makes possible a deep sharing can have this power.

One man described a time in his parish when they had all become stagnant. There was no growth of any kind. He was depressed and the members of the congregation were looking about for someone or something to blame. In religious studies this is called divination: to find the source of evil, which is assumed to be external to ourselves, and to eliminate it. On occasion in the past it took the form of searching out and burning witches. One evening when the pastor met with his board he tried for something different, revelation through prayer.

For fifteen minutes they sat in *silent* prayer. Silence, as we know, is very threatening to many people.

> Somebody finally felt called upon to articulate some things in prayer, and they were not people who normally would have done that. I didn't have to say anything. I felt that was a great beginning. A sense of tension went out of me. In the very best sense of the word I would say it was a charismatic experience. There was a real sense of calm. This [shared prayer] went on for about a half an hour. That set a new tone which was picked up by the rest of the congregation on subsequent Sundays.

Out of this experience came a program of vestry visitation that has now become a norm in the parish for mutual visitation by the entire membership. A new life has come into that parish and into this pastor.

A young priest, who had not been ordained for very long and tended therefore to sound just a bit like a textbook, spoke of his expectations that he would discover the Christ in the situations of his pastoral ministry. "Sometimes I find in my work in the parish," he said, "if I am a kind of wasteland spiritually, God works very significantly in this person [to whom I am ministering]." Then he went on to add, "God works in incarnational community. I have faith this is where I will grow. You grow holy by what you do."

Essentially the conviction of this priest that you grow holy by what you are doing in the parish sums up the experience of many of those men and women interviewed for this study. But it is a doing with the intention of discerning Christ there in a particular event. Therefore, those occasions that are fraught with transcendent implications—the sacraments, personal crises, parish conflicts—have the greatest potential for drawing the ordained person into an awareness of his or her vocation. For as we bear the pain of those we serve—what Charles Williams named coinherence—our life is as broken open as theirs is. In its openness we see the divine purpose, working its effect upon our vision of the world.

Scheduling Prayer

There is probably no subject on which there was a wider range of opinion among those interviewed than the ability and desirability of scheduling a time each day for prayer and study. The idea of a regular discipline created resentment in a few. This was perhaps the clearest expression of that feeling:

> I have a negative image of spiritual discipline in terms of what the seminary tried to lay on us of a disciplined life of prayer, meditation, study—telling us examples of others who got up at four or five in the morning and prayed for two or three hours.

A moderated response, which was part of a reflection upon a life of steady personal growth, was that discipline changed with the ebb and flow of life.

> I've never had a real rigid [schedule of] reading the morning prayer book, or anything like that sort of thing. We had our devotions at the breakfast table with the children. To speak of a disciplined something you're going to do regardless—this has not been part of my experience. There will be times I will be spending a lot of time reading, meditating, and this kind of thing; there will be other times it just hasn't happened that way.

In those persons interviewed who rejected the need for a systematic commitment to a daily schedule there was, at the same time, the belief that their parish routine needed to be lived in a conscious relationship to God. This observation spoke to that in an effective manner:

> A disciplined life to me doesn't mean keeping rules anymore. It means keeping recollected what I am and what I am for, I think. In every context of life I try to remember that.

But there are also those clergy who make a very strong case for the relationship of rules to the recollective life. One priest spoke of the danger of always living on the superficial level and the need to break through the surface to get a glimpse of the reality beyond. "Access [to that deeper reality]," he said, "to me requires me to have a regular discipline." Another said that his daily rosary, meditation, and Eucharist were crucial to his spiritual nurture. One pastor elaborated what keeping rules meant to him:

It [spirituality] has some elements of sacrifice in Discipline would be an important word in that area of spirituality. Discipline has to do with a rather intentional kind of spiritual strengthening which has to do with Bible study, some time in a week or a day for prayer, for meditation. There is a physical side as well, which is very important; in other words, exercise.

No one claimed that it is easy for the parish pastor to shape his day to allow for a regular life of prayer and reading. This priest spoke of the problem for him and, at the same time, his commitment:

I wish I had the time. I do my best. Necessary is a certain time of mental prayer and spiritual reading, with also the theological reading to continue on studying, broadening one's vision of the spiritual life and the means for salvation.

Several of those persons interviewed had gone to the same seminary. Each spontaneously mentioned a faculty member who had a lasting effect upon their own image as a pastor with an intentional prayer life. They described him as a man of high principle, disciplined, and deeply committed to the study of the Scriptures in the very best sense of that word. They went on to say that he was not the kind of man you would invite over for a drink. Apparently they preferred to admire him from afar. There is a hint here of a longing to be doing better than they were, but an unwillingness to make the sacrifice.

It is interesting to contrast the responses in the interview to the question on the Spiritual Style Inventory: "A disciplined daily routine of prayer, with specific goals and objectives, is . . ." The overall mean would indicate that for our sample it is "usually important" (3.9 on a scale of 1 to 5, n = 16). Here the denominational breakdown is suggestive although it must be kept in mind that the sample is very small for each denomination. The Roman Catholics score a 4.5 (n = 4), the Episcopalians a 4.2 (n = 6), the Lutherans a 3.8 (n = 3), and the Presbyterians a 3.0 (n = 3). My guess is that the attitude on this subject has to do with socialization and the continuing support of that action. The Roman Catholics with the tradition of the daily Eucharist and the influence of the religious life on secular clergy have a strong tradition, as do the Episcopalians with the daily office. But no denomination as a whole would appear to dismiss the importance of a life of scheduled, daily personal prayer for its clergy.

There is probably nowhere in the life of the parish priest or pastor that the question of priorities confronts us so plainly. It would probably be wrong for us to single out the clergy as a class and say that they have failed in their obligation to pray regularly and without ceasing (1 Thess. 5:17). Prayer is not the unique responsibility of the ordained, and many of the spiritual masters of the Christian tradition were lay persons. But the instrumental responsibility of the clergy is evident, and it is doubtful that we can expect a church to pray whose priests and pastors fail to pray regularly.

In the research for this book I spoke with a couple of persons who as a part of their ministry conduct regional conferences for ordained persons and laity in the life of prayer. In doing this they get an overview of what is happening in the parishes throughout the country. Their sense is that people come to their priest or pastor seeking spiritual growth and are frequently given poor advice. Often they are given books to read that just confuse them—they cannot even understand the language—and they are left unfed. It is no wonder that many of these people chase after strange gurus and join esoteric sects. The impression that accompanies this inept pastoral assistance is that if the ordained persons prayed regularly they would know to help the people they serve with simple, practical advice.

What I mean by simple, practical advice is nothing more than this: to tell the person what I have found helpful in my life, and to show them how I do it and when I do it. Then having done that—*and this is most important*—I say that this is only one way to pray and to be more aware of God, and that there are other ways. Then I should be able to name a few of those ways and give the names and whereabouts of those who could help them in those ways. The point is that we cannot help people pray if we do not pray ourselves; and, furthermore, ordination presents people with the assumption that we are there to help them pray.

Historically the church has identified prayer with a daily routine. The daily office—a service of Bible reading, psalms and canticles, and brief intercessions and petitions—emerged very early in pious Christian homes. It was adopted in the cenobitic religious life in the third and fourth centuries and eventually developed into the "seven monastic hours," said to be in conformity with the psalmist who declared, "Seven times a day I praise thee for the justice of thy decrees" (Psalm 119:164). The Eastern tradition of the "breath prayer" as a way of praying unceasingly developed by the fourth century and is very much alive today.

When over a period of several centuries the invasions of the Roman Empire by tribes from the north radically changed European civilization, the shape of Christian piety tended to become more simple in accordance with what could be expected of clergy and laity alike. Reading, meditation or reflection, and prayer was the threefold pattern taught for centuries in monastery and parish. In an illiterate society, where books were a rare and priceless commodity, the Scriptures and the lives of the saints were read aloud to the hearers. This made for a very different kind of response to the Word than we make today. Auricular learning, unlike visual learning, comprehends reality not as a logical sequence, but as an interrelated whole. It is much more in accord with the imagination than logic. We need to keep in mind that those who wrote the Bible, for example, never thought that it would be used except to be read out loud.

Henri Nouwen in *Reaching Out* wrote, "without the Bible, without silent time and without someone to direct us, finding our way to God is very hard and practically impossible."[5] Nouwen's simple rules are an adaptation of the medieval pattern. They are in accord with the spiritual style of those interviewed. For them mental prayer comes more naturally than vocal prayer and silence is a necessity.

Mental prayer is a rumination with God. It has as its purpose getting to know God better and letting God know us better. If we can rid ourselves of the negative connotation of the expression, it is a form of "small talk"—but small talk with a clear intention of being an exercise in joint imaginations. It is from the methodologies of Ignatius Loyola, Francis de Sales, Jean-Jacques Olier, and others, to nothing more than the "free, more penetrating gaze of mind" upon God characteristic of contemplation. Vocal prayer is classically the Lord's Prayer, the Hail Mary, the *Gloria patri*, and all the carefully composed prayers of liturgies, free worship, or private devotion.

Not infrequently those clergy interviewed spoke of intercession lists they keep and use daily. These pastors take seriously the expectations and requests of their people to pray for them. One man makes a point of mentioning to his parishioners that he prayed for them today, yesterday, or the day before. But the heart of the prayer life for most of the priests and pastors is mental prayer. It is more consistent with a recollected life—one in which the presence of God through the day is purposely and gently brought to mind. This conforms with the admonition of Teresa of Avila to her nuns:

> Insofar as I can understand, the gate of entry to this [interior] castle is prayer and reflection. I don't mean to refer to mental more than vocal prayer, for since vocal prayer is prayer it must be accompanied by reflection. A prayer in which a person is not aware of whom he is speaking to, what he is asking, who it is who is asking and of whom, I do not call prayer however much the lips may move.[6]

In this translation "prayer" apparently means vocal prayer and "reflection" means mental prayer.

Silence was almost universally sought by those interviewed, although occasionally it was seen as an avoidance of human interaction. One typical remark was that silence is "very important to me; I don't get as much of it as I would like." When asked why silence is a threat to so many people, this same priest replied, "In silence you really encounter God, and if you are afraid of that encounter you are going to avoid silence like the plague."

Whether we think about it historically or consider it phenomenologically, it is not possible to conceive of an intentional spiritual discipline, without some form of regular, scheduled prayer. Remember that the definition of prayer is very broad in this study. The point is to set aside time to be wittingly with God. The reasons given for not making this a top priority by those who argued against such an intentional time were hollow and had a guilty ring. I sensed this because it picked up that piece of me that would like to think that one can have a close walk with God and not purposely spend some time each day with him. I felt the guilt in me when I identified with them.

The simple fact is that busy priests and pastors can get up at five in the morning to pray. At least one of those interviewed, a wife and mother who shares a parish with her husband, does just that. She keeps a journal, she reads the Scriptures, she is silent, and she prays. I doubt that there is anyone in whom this unfailing practice is more evident in the character of her life. She is a woman of great depth, sacrificial compassion, and sensitivity to social injustice.

A priest who spoke of reading the daily offices and of spending an hour a day in private prayer described his priorities this way:

> I have some priorities set up that I operate on. My first priority is God and what's happening there—my really listening to

him and trying to walk through the day with him. Second, I try to focus on—which is really the hardest area—my own mental, physical, and spiritual health, but that often gets shortchanged. And third, I try to be a good member of my family. And fourth, I put the parish there because the parish always ends up in first place anyway; so I put it down at the end and let it fall back into that place and I push it back down and it emerges again.

Those are priorities that are worth keeping before us: God, self, family, and parish. The man who shared them with me is someone who has a sense of proportion born of detachment, discretion, and discernment, which enables him to pray intentionally without being tyrannized by his rule.

One cannot have a life of recollection, that is, a sense of walking through the day in the company of God, without periods that focus specifically upon our relationship with God. We do not pray because we feel like praying, we pray because we know that this is a fulfillment of our vocation: to live as spiritual beings.

Conclusion

The piety of the parish pastor informs his or her ministry with the congregation, discovers those occasions of illumination within the life of the congregation, and is lived in tension with the demands of the congregation. The vocation of the ordained person is neither a mere projection of the parish's calling nor is it a gift to him or her alone, allowing the individual to be indifferent to congregational life. The call to serve as priest or pastor is both internal and external—a matter of one's individual inner awareness and the ratification of that awareness by the church—and should manifest itself in the living out of that vocation through a lifetime.

Many a pastor is dashed against one of two sets of rocks. He or she comes to be a hired flunky, on the one hand, a functionary chaplain to the establishment, or, on the other hand, he or she assumes the role of a petulant adolescent, working out his or her hostility upon the unwitting congregation. We excuse the former on the grounds that we are pastors, and we argue for the latter by claiming to be prophets. The truth of the matter is often neither one nor the other, but that we are spiritually bankrupt.

The dangers of these alternative courses to disaster are relatively well known in ministry studies. The solutions found in continuing education, consultation, and career evaluation are valuable, but they can easily lack the one ingredient essential to the vocation: a growing awareness of God's purpose for us. The intention is to live as a symbol and symbol-bearer of that which transcends as well as incorporates our secular expertise. This cannot be accomplished unless we steer through the straits between these Scylla and Charybdis of ministry guided by a living relationship with the Lord we profess to serve.

IV. The Support

10. Spiritual Companionship

ONE OF the surprises at first glance in this study came out of the Myers-Briggs inventory, which measures conscious psychological types according to the categories of analytical psychology. Fifty percent of the sample (eight out of sixteen), scored as extroverted intuitives. Sheldon Kopp describes the extroverted intuitive as follows:

> Like General Custer, other extreme Extroverted Intuitive Types are often appealingly passionate, impulsive rascals who enliven any situation they come upon, wreak romantic havoc, and often come to a bad end. More moderate examples of such types lack such intense colorfulness but are also focused on their own intuitive hunches about external events. Their ability to see hidden possibilities and focus on the new and promising often makes them competent promoters, enthusiastic advance men, and sharp speculators.[1]

My guess is that the disproportionate number of extroverted intuitive types in this sample results from the fact that it is parish clergy who are being examined. To be an effective pastor of a congregation one needs to be oriented toward the external world of other people. But the spiritual life demands an interest in the hidden truth that requires a keen intuitive capacity to uncover. The problems of this type include a proclivity to be easily bored and an insensitivity to the practicalities of a situation.

If this book had sought out for study spiritually mature persons who were religious or who were members of the academic community, my suspicion is that more introverted intuitives would have

shown up. Such persons are more inclined than the extroverted intuitives to live by their own internal story in ways that do not demand a
wide range of interpersonal relationships. But it is the parish clergy
who interest us here and is to their needs for spiritual companionship
that this final chapter attempts to speak.

Another interesting discovery in exploring the clergy sample
was that in Hopewell's worldview inventory, they scored heavily empiric. This outlook relies upon data objectively verifiable through
one's five senses, with emphasis placed upon personal integrity and
a premium put upon being realistic and responsible. The least represented worldview was the gnostic, which, surprisingly enough, relies upon esoteric wisdom and inner awareness. My expectation was
that the gnostic worldview would have scored higher among a group
so strongly intuitive.

Upon reflection, however, there is a hint of the problem that faces
the spirituality of the parish priest or pastor—even those identified as
"mature"—in the contrast between the findings of the Myers-Briggs
inventory and the Hopewell inventory. Here is someone who is most
comfortable as the knight errant, always seeking the new in the world
about him or her, who has been socialized to trust only the five senses
and to expect to be held accountable to whatever he or she claims is
real. The professional model of the ordained person, the heavy reliance upon the behavioral and functional models in the human sciences in ministry studies, and the distrust of theology that
characterizes many contemporary clergy are symptomatic of the need
to fulfill the self-imposed expectations of an empiric worldview. We are
all a bit skeptical of much else.

Clergy as a class are not good at the use of time. We find it difficult to say no. We feel a need to justify what we are doing as worthwhile, not only to others but to ourselves. My guess is that this is a
result of our acceptance of the empiric worldview, with its valuing of
integrity based upon demonstrable merit. This immediately confronts
us with a source of frustration, for aside from all else the heart of the
vocation of the priest or pastor is not subject to empirical verification.

But the conflict is deeper than this. For lurking beneath the surface
in many an ordained person is the suspicion that he who calls us speaks
in ways to which our empirical self is deaf. This conflict is not just a
matter of meeting external expectations; it is a question of reconciling
our own intuitive proclivities with a lifetime of being pragmatic. We
know that the professional model is inadequate, we are aware that the

human sciences fall short of describing our experience, and we would like to be theologically astute. But it is immensely difficult to identify what it is that ferrets out the hidden possibilities in our experience that go beyond mere observation, much less to have the courage to live our life by the light of this inner awareness.

Clergy are a guilty lot. We are torn between our fondness for the adventure of intuitive insight and the need to justify ourselves empirically. Frustration turns into anger and scepticism becomes cynicism. We fall into that hallowed American custom of solving our dilemma by working just that much harder, which is exacerbated by the expectation that we are an unceasing source of love, compassion, tenderness, and comfort. That which feeds the pastor is passed over, largely because we think we need to spend the time making evident our own value to the people who expect our ministry. We become burned out, bored, disillusioned, and guilty over our failure.

Many clergy have the idea that an important way of preventing burnout is to develop a support group, in which ordained persons share and feed one another. My own belief is that this is a move in the right direction, but not always a satisfactory solution. Some groups reinforce the hostility and self-pity to which some clergy are given. Ventilation for its own sake is of little value. Other groups avoid the issues of vocation in the name of being members of the "helping professions," as in the case of doctors, nurses, clinical psychologists, and social workers. This only obscures the need to identify what it means to be ordained, which is ultimately outside the ken of the human sciences.

In my judgment we are far more likely to deal with the intrapsychic and the institutional conflicts between the inner awareness of vocation and the expectations of demonstrable value when we allow ourselves to be confronted by the issue of the state of our own spirit. The issues of clerical guilt and anger are fundamentally spiritual questions from the pain of whose resolution we guard ourselves by a cynicism justified through empiricism.

What is called for is a spiritual companionship, in which in some configuration we are willing to be confronted at the point of our life of prayer. In my research I had the hunch more than once that this was dismissed as a personal impossibility on the convenient grounds that one particular form of spiritual companionship was objectionable or that no one that met our expectations of perfection was available. Here I am arguing for the necessity of spiritual companionship as a principle. What shape it takes is a matter of historical happenstance.

The Renewal Movement

One form of spiritual companionship comes in the support from enthusiastic prayer groups. Dennis Bennett, an early leader in the contemporary charismatic movement, preached at the Episcopal chapel at Louisiana State University in Baton Rouge in the early sixties when I was there. I remember well his vivid description of what the charismatic experience meant to him. Up until the time of his "being baptized in the Holy Spirit," he said, ministry was for him like perpetually taxiing down a runway and never taking off. Once he had the charismatic experience, he "took off." It is a helpful simile, if we keep in mind the problem of clergy burnout. Our expectations born of a secular worldview often never get us beyond continual taxiing, which eventually becomes extremely boring.

Bennett speaks for many clergy who in their desire to fulfill their intuition of vocation sought—sometimes quite unconsciously—and achieved a radical break from the inherited cultural perception of reality. There are certainly those who think if any genuine spiritual renewal is to take place in Western culture it will require just this kind of dramatic subversion of the normal secular outlook with its presupposition that God does not reveal himself to us today.

Among the clergy interviewed there were a significant minority who had experienced charismatic renewal. For them it provided the kind of spiritual companionship they needed at a point in their life. But in almost every case this recollection of their charismatic experience was one of gratitude, tempered by a distance born of time. This was especially true of one priest, who said with great appreciation:

> I was introduced to an adult spirituality through the charismatic movement and brought into it with all that I have. That was my conversion, certainly my encounter with the person of the Holy Spirit.

What followed this comment was a touching reminiscence of life in several prayer groups and even an attempt at communal living. He spoke of harassing his parish priest, who had resisted the enthusiasm of this group, and going back years later to apologize. Then he went on to add:

> The charismatic business was the skeleton for me to which a lot of things were added. [Now I'm] to the point where I'm

not involved in anything directly charismatic and have my own issues with them. Here in this community we have "the one true perfect church," which has just been established. I've been there. It isn't going to work. I'm not really majoring in anything charismatic now.

Two clergy, neither of whom had been ordained for more than three or four years, were influenced in their vocational decision by their charismatic experience. Both were only slightly qualified in their evaluation of what had happened to them. One, a Roman Catholic, said:

The charismatic movement was very significant for the historical development of the church. I was in the movement myself. I think it's providential in terms of creating a Holy Spirit dimension and appreciation for the teachings of Vatican II, which mentions the Holy Spirit all over the place. I think that movement has given a life and fellowship to Catholics and other Christians as well. It has given many people a new experience of small group fellowship. [It has] given them a great experience that they can read the Bible and be nourished by it and be inspired by it.

He went on to note that occasionally the charismatic movement is thought to be cliquish and lacking in social concern, but he considered this only "partially true."

I was struck by how similar the vocational struggle of this Roman Catholic priest was to a Lutheran pastor who spoke of his charismatic experience in this way:

It's been like a romance which started out real hot and passionate. I've been drawn to it at different places, but then I floated away from it. I'm back now to where I can see its place in the church.

He too mentioned that the charismatic movement is afraid of theology and is given to literalism. An example of their theological naïveté, he reported, is the belief in the rapture. He considered it his task as part of the movement to elevate their theological vision.

The results of the Myers-Briggs inventory are almost identical in all three of these men. Two are extroverted intuitives, with feeling and perceiving (ENFP), and one is an extroverted intuitive, with feeling and judging (ENFJ). The last named is Roman Catholic, and is characteristic of all four Roman Catholics in our sample, who show a preference for structure over spontaneity (i.e., judging over perceiving). Perhaps the preference for evaluation by feeling rather than analytical thinking is important in these profiles, particularly when combined with intuition.

In the Hopewell worldview inventory all three men quoted preferred an empiric outlook and the charismatic ranked no higher than third. My suspicion is, however, that the expectations of the charismatic movement are not necessarily the same as what Hopewell means by "charismatic": a reliance upon the personally perceived evidence of God's immanence. There is a stronger sense in the charismatic movement of the "invasion" of the world by God's transcendence and consequently an emphasis upon a God who acts *ad hoc*.

On this basis it would appear that for some priests and pastors the charismatic movement has provided a helpful spiritual companionship along the way, but it is not such a consuming passion in their journey that its point of view radically changes the predominant cultural outlook. Someone of an intuitive nature would be open to the experience of enthusiasm, but the experience is placed within a larger need to be accountable to our five senses. At least in this sample there is no wholesale repudiation of the prevailing way of making sense of life. These people are not given to literalism.

Even for those clerics in the research sample who have not had a clear charismatic experience, the evaluation of the movement is mostly positive, which is indicative of the flexibility and openness of the spiritually mature. One Roman Catholic priest spoke of a Thursday night meeting with a group in his parish, which always begins with the Eucharist. As he put it, he emphasizes to them attendance at Mass, devotion to the Blessed Mother, and absolute loyalty to the church, and then gives thanks for this enthusiasm. Another pastor remarked that he knows too many rational, sane people who have become charismatics to write it off. Still another priest describes it as a real breakthrough.

But there was some rather strong negative evaluation as well, which may boil down to who we are and what our past exposure to the movement has been. These remarks from a Methodist pastor—a representative of *the* American enthusiastic tradition—are interesting.

My experience with the charismatic movement has been one of disillusionment, fear, a feeling they have nothing to offer me. Even in its milder form I have yet to see anyone who is able to sustain any kind of relationship to the church. I think it has a lot of built-in elitism, a great, great concentration of tension and feelings, and a pietism which doesn't have any other spiritual outlet. [I'm] very negative. I'm sure there must be some good charismatics; I just haven't found any of them.

A Lutheran—Luther himself tried to suppress enthusiasm—adds his own perspective:

> Frankly, they don't know what it's all about. We've lost three pastors to it. It caused terrible strife in their congregations. Because these congregations are no dumb clucks, they know what's going on. But these fellows were not grounded [in theology]. [It] used to be that I said in seminary that the fellows who were not grounded in theology went into the liturgical movement, but now I say those who are not grounded in theology go into the charismatic movement. Anyone who has ever read Luther's dealings with the Schwärmer—anyone who understands that and understands why he was so upset about it can understand the whole charismatic movement.

The Lutheran pastor is an extroverted sensation type on the Myers-Briggs, with neither thinking nor feeling dominant and with a very strong desire for structure (ES-J). The expectation would be that he is concerned for objects and concrete facts. All this comes out in his obvious distress over disturbances within congregations and his commitment to solid theology that defines what the church is.

The charismatic movement is only the widest known of a number of renewal movements that are present in the church today; others are marriage encounter, the cursillo movement, and that constellation of lay witness groups of which "Faith Alive" is an example. There is no doubt that these movements, as well as the charismatic movement, often provide access to spiritual companionship that is not available otherwise. It is also true that there is always a risk of the contamination of our spirituality with some odd notions, inasmuch as enthusiastic movements are usually theologically tone-deaf and historically naive.

This explains one criticism of them in the research sample, namely, that they thwart continued spiritual growth. People get "hung up" at one point in their development. When they do continue to grow spiritually, they go beyond the movement and find a greater degree of theological and historical sophistication.

This suggests that enthusiastic groups, such as the charismatic movement, serve a purpose for some people at one point in their spiritual journey. The unfortunate truth seems to be, however, that this happens at a price that would not have to be paid if the church itself were less inclined to reflect the presuppositions concerning God's presence in his world found in the secular society. Spiritual companionship could then spring from the heart of the church.

The Friend of the Soul

Historically, spiritual companionship in premodern Christianity has been typified in the form of the soul friend. No question in the interviews of clergy brought forth a greater sense of ambivalence than the one pertaining to the use and qualifications of such a spiritual guide, friend, director, companion, or what-have-you. Certain titles such as spiritual director provoked ambiguous feelings. One pastor observed that he was not interested in having a spiritual "guide or director," for apparently the name connoted a kind of subservience to which he was not inclined; but he went on to say, "I seek a person I can relate to and interact with and share, because I need a support community that is intimate enough to provide me some spiritual resources." The question that remains is what is meant by "spiritual resources."

There is no doubt that there is a negative communal memory of the tyrannical spiritual director, to whom the hapless individual surrendered his whole will. This memory has been remarkably long lasting, for it comes out of the practice of the late Middle Ages and early modern period and bears only a remote relationship to what went before and no necessary connection to what is needed now. It was Aelred of Rievaulx (1109–1197), a Cistercian monk from northern England and the son of a priest, who wrote a treatise *On Spiritual Friendship*, based upon Cicero's essay on friendship, and who initially stimulated thinking about the friend of the soul. There is little in Aelred that provokes a strong negative response and there is some material in his treatise very much in the spirit of what those interviewed for this study spoke of wanting.

The perceived importance of having a spiritual director per se seems directly related to denominational background. Episcopalians apparently think one is most important (4.7 on a scale of 1 to 5), Roman Catholics almost as important (4.3), and then are followed by Lutherans (3.7), and Presbyterians (1.7). But the interviews would indicate that these statistics can be deceptive. If they say anything they point to an intention to go and find someone called a "spiritual director." Almost everyone welcomes a friend who may emerge in the course of our life together and with whom we can share our spiritual journey.

One pastor summed up what all seemed to want: "I hunger for that [friendship of the soul] and I don't find it as often [as I might wish]." The hunger of which he is speaking is for a person to be and do a combination of things. We want someone with whom we can test where we are in the spiritual journey—to get a kind of navigational fix—someone with whom we can find solace in times of great stress, check out pastoral decisions, tap for new ideas or directions, and make our confession. Among both Roman Catholics and Episcopalians there seemed to be no particular distinction between a friend of the soul and a confessor, who are not the same thing. (A confessor deals with guilt provoked by identifiable acts of sin; a friend of the soul relates to a pervasive guilt born of our antique alienation from God.) The desire for a friend of the soul lacked much clear focus, and the hunger was more for companionship than for particular services from another person.

The opacity of intention in the hunger for a spiritual companion exists in direct proportion to the lack of definition in one's spiritual theology. The discussions of the friend of the soul were not generally discursive and sometimes were fairly guilt-laden. I relate this to a resistance to hard thinking in the area of the spiritual life, if not also to a confusion as to how one would go about doing something about it. It seemed at times that those interviewed almost wished the Holy Spirit would simply seize them in some charismatic experience and relieve them of the pain of knowing that they should be more intentional about their prayer life than they were. In all fairness, there is not much in parish life that would provide definition to their spiritual theology much less lead them to do anything but wish for a greater spiritual vision.

One way, of course, of doing something about the confusion in one's prayer life is to seek out a competent friend of the soul. The initial point made by even the most desirous is that such persons are rare indeed. One person said, "I'm looking for a wise, old man," but he gave the nonexistence of such persons in his area as the reason he had no spiritual guide. Another priest, who was clearer than most about what constituted for him a friend of the soul, simply said that when he came to the part of the country in which he now served he had to give up having a spiritual guide because no one was available. Several of those interviewed who spoke of having directors, with one notable exception, implied that they had decided to settle for what they could get. Others seemed to be waiting for someone simply to arise. As one man put it, "it is probably better to let them arrive like the sun and the rain and the dew, as sent by the Lord."

What do people want in the person who becomes a friend of the soul? The answers include greater spiritual maturity, the obvious presence in them of the Spirit, a willingness to listen, a liberal amount of holiness, compassion, a total commitment to the other person's needs, an inability to be shocked, compatibility, honesty, confidentiality, and kindness. Several statements struck me. One very skilled spiritual director replied to my question of what he looked for in a friend of the soul: "I personally would look for someone who when I met with them and spoke with them my heart leapt." One pastor used C. S. Lewis as a model, because he said, he was "thoroughly converted. He would not give up in trying to make the Christian faith fit in his life. He kept making things come together." Someone else suggested:

> I look for somebody who will let me be myself in faith, who appreciates the uniqueness of the person, who is very much relating my life and the life in Christ, but giving me a tremendous amount of freedom to be myself in faith.

This man, incidentally, was the one who spoke most warmly of the friend of his soul.

Perhaps saddest was the feeling—explicit in one or two, implicit in more—that church politics really stood in the way of an effective spiritual companionship. Tragically there is evidence of the inability of clergy to keep confidences, which is an unspeakable violation of one's ordination. It undermines any possibility of being an effective friend of the soul. Envy creeps into far too many collegial conversations, isolating the ordained from one another and creating a climate of suspicion and despair. One pastor spoke of his search for a spiritual guide:

I looked for someone who would be kind, would try to un-derstand where I was coming from whatever I came to him with, someone who was wise in all senses of that word, some-one who would keep everything I said in absolute confi-dence, someone who would share himself with me. Unfortunately our polity really does not encourage the total baring of one's soul and one's feelings and the confessing of one's sins.

The result was that he had to go outside his own tradition to find a friend of his soul.

Despite the fact that almost every person interviewed denied that there was a difference between clerical and lay spirituality, most of them thought of a friend of the soul as ordained and male. There ap-pears to be a disparity between what we profess about the nature of spirituality and what we feel comfortable practicing. Obviously there are clergy who use lay persons, including women, as spiritual guides, but this did not seem to be the rule in this particular sample. One man did describe a woman who was, as he put it, his self-appointed direc-tor. He acknowledged that she was usually "on target," but he was ap-parently not willing to seek her out on a regular basis.

I discovered in the research for this study that, as often seems to be the case, there is a longing for some form of spiritual companion-ship, but what that looks like is obscured by a great deal of personal history and disappointment. As I listened I thought of what I under-stand to be my function when I serve as a friend of someone's soul. It is to share in another's particular pilgrimage. That journey is of neces-sity an inner exploration, so I seek to help a person identify his or her internal experience and relate it to the Gospel and its explication in the Christian tradition. This requires me to be informed by reading the Scriptures and the spiritual masters. I want to clarify what is hap-pening to that person historically and phenomenologically, and in do-ing this I expect that my friend will both find room to develop his or her own unique style and will discern a particular direction in which he or she is moving by God's intention. Behind all of this lies the as-sumption that to be human is to be spiritual in the sense that I have defined it in this book.

To be a spiritual friend one must have detachment, discretion, and discernment, with all that prepares for those gifts. Spiritual com-panionship is a gentle art, demanding a willingness to listen as if one had a third ear attuned to the inner self. It is neither psychotherapy nor is it the sacrament of reconciliation. Sometimes one needs to confront, but far more often the best intervention of the spiritual guide is in parabolic language, nudging the friend into a new way of seeing. The journey belongs to the other and that person's uniqueness must always be honored.

The friend of the soul is an instrumental image. Such a person is not to be a "buddy," but someone who listens, comforts, and supports. He or she serves as a hermeneut, which means that he or she is a means, not an end. It is important for me not to think too highly of myself in this relationship, but to stand in awe of what God is doing in the life of the other person. Often this requires me to get out of the way. When in ignorance I have nothing to say, I must remain silent.

In a previous book[2] I wrote of the priest as a "wagon master" in the days of the American western frontier. His qualification was that he had been over the trail before, he knew where the water holes were and where the Indians might attack. The wagon master did not drive the wagons and all the travelers had to shoot for themselves. Each person's motives for being on that quest were their own and not his business. He had courage and commitment, but there were no guarantees of getting to California. I think it is still a good image and when I am a friend of the soul I think of myself as the wagon master of the other's inner journey.

A Prescription

In the months of doing research and writing this book the question that has occasionally sprung up in conversation and persists in my mind is one of *accountability*: To whom or to what is the ordained person accountable? The pious (and true) answer is God. Enthusiasm, particularly in its contemporary form of pietism, often wants to leave the answer at that point. But those of us who believe in the Incarnation know that God never reveals himself as some ethereal abstraction or inner feeling of personal worthiness, as convenient as that might be when we want to escape him. He came to us in the human form of Jesus of Nazareth, and he continues to come to his church, her word, and sacraments. Accountability in Christian theology is concrete, specific, responsive, and discriminating.

Another answer other than God to the question of to whom I am accountable might be myself. This response is naive. Most, if not all, of us are better able to fool ourselves than anyone else. From the psychotic mystic to the faithless pastor, self-justification is very easy. It is for this reason that the Christian life is corporate, requiring collaboration.

It would appear that even the spiritually mature clergy of today have ambivalent feelings about accountability, particularly as it relates to the life of prayer. To varying degrees we want it, but we do not want it. Spiritual companionship is at heart a form of accountability that has become objectified. It is outside ourselves and not subject to our inner procrastination. We can often kid ourselves—for example, "Prayer characterizes my day and I need no specific time," or "There is no time in my day for silence"—but a good spiritual companion knows our excuses for what they are and reminds us of the painful truth.

In the less structured conversations with ordained persons about this research—those who were not necessarily "into prayer"—the value for them of being "confused about spirituality" was obvious. Clergy do not have to be held accountable for what other people cannot make clear to them. Yet there remains in them a lingering guilt, associated with a diffused anger. It underlies the discussion of their own vocation and its relationship to the so-called helping professions. It was rare, however, that an honest conversation about the secularization of the ordained ministry could be separated from the barbed humor that characteristically hides both the hurt and the insecurity of too many clergy.

It is altogether remarkable that priests and pastors can become so inarticulate on the subject of the heart of their vocation: its relation to the spiritual life. I recall a woman who was the chairperson of a parish search committee telling me that her bishop suggested one question to ask prospective pastors: "Do you believe in God?" She was amazed at this advice, but followed it. I asked her what she found out and her reply was that, while all candidates said they did, she concluded that some in fact did not believe in God.

A nonnegotiable assumption in my judgment is not only that the ordained person believes in God, but that he or she seeks a relationship with God. Any other idea renders the notion of vocation absurd. The conversation begins with what it means to be on that quest. The pivotal point of this study's definition of spirituality is the broadened or heightened consciousness as the gift of our relationship with God. In one sense this is what is meant by *knowing* God: sharing his vision for creation. There is no methodology for guaranteeing that such a new consciousness will be forthcoming, but there are two thousand years of Christian teaching on how to become vulnerable to the possibility of such knowledge.

My prescription, which begins with accountability to a specific, concrete, responsive, and discriminating other, is for becoming vulnerable.

What we are accountable *for* is our rule. It is not so important what our rule is, but that we have one. The word comes from the Latin *regula*, which means a straightedge, something we use to measure our conduct. It is not a cause of tyranny, as those who wish to argue against having a rule sometimes suggest, but quite the opposite. It is an expression of our intentions that liberates us from the tyranny of our feelings. There is nothing quite so mindlessly autocratic as our endocrine glands, and I personally abhor that devotion to them in the name of "getting in touch with our feelings." Knowing how we feel is important, but being responsible for our feelings is vital. A rule is simply a statement of what we intend to do in order to achieve a posture of vulnerability to God's illuminating presence.

The source of that rule, as well as the accountability for its exercise, can be our spiritual companion. Such a companion can take several forms. Roman Catholic clergy in the religious orders are provided a rule to which their members are held accountable. This practice flows over into the secular clergy as well. Episcopalians are given to devotional societies, some of which are adjuncts of religious orders, which offer the parish clergy rules of varying shape and rigor. Every Episcopalian I interviewed, with one exception, had some relationship to a religious order now or in the past. For the Presbyterians, Lutherans, and Methodists I interviewed the tradition of the devotional society was either remote or absent. Of course, there is no reason why that has to be true, and there are resources available.

There is no reason why a rule cannot be worked out between two people, one to one, and be something entirely individual. James Fenhagen's deceptively simple little book *More Than Wanderers*[3] provides an excellent beginning point for those who feel a bit awkward about starting.

What I think any good rule should include is: (1) reading of Scripture and Christian spiritual classics, (2) a time of solitude and silence (i.e., being alone with God in a posture of listening), (3) vocal prayer (a good test of our vision is the nature of our intercessions and petitions), and (4) provision for an ongoing plan of action. There should be room in every rule for our own distinctive style. For example, some persons prefer apophatic forms of meditation such as the "Jesus prayer," while others find the Ignatian method better. There are those who will keep intercession lists, while some clergy find that this gets in the way. Particular denominational emphases I have left unmentioned, such as the sacrament of reconciliation, but they need to be included where appropriate. My assumption is that all of this is rooted in eucharistic worship.

Rules should be simple, but their simplicity should not fool us. Our rule is the primary point at which we claim a specific and concrete responsibility for living that life of prayer discussed in this book. In our accountability for our rule we are continually reminded of the transcendent nature of our vocation and the need to weigh the implications of that call for the manner of our life. The rule and its accountability become the catalyst for the recollective life, which colors the thoughts and actions of the priest and pastor and gives his instrumentality that authenticity and translucent quality that is appropriate to the symbol and symbol-bearer.

Conclusion

Gregory of Nyssa uses the following image to describe the ordained person:

> In the fruit that Aaron's rod produced it is fitting to perceive the kind of life that must characterize the priesthood—namely, a life self-controlled, tough and dried in appearance, but containing on the inside (hidden and invisible) what can be eaten. It becomes visible when the food ripens and the hard shell is stripped off and the wood-like covering of the meat is removed.[4]

A contemporary parallel for Gregory's self-control is intention. An intention is known by its goal, the final cause of our actions. The actions themselves are the deliberate decisions of the whole person, constituted in acts of will, to make that goal an actuality.

Our goal is the Kingdom, the completion of God's creative vision, and we are God's hands in bringing that to pass. Those hands must touch the lives of those we serve at the point of their deepest heartfelt and most profound longing. The pastor is truly called to live with people at the level of their ultimate issues and values, as in matters of sexuality, vocation, birth, and death. In the final analysis, what can be more worthwhile? Why do we have to pander to false models?

We cannot pretend to be such instruments, however, if we do not renounce what would distract us from such a delicate caring. We have to be tough. Satan would have us serve another god. We may appear to be dried, for there is not much energy left for cosmetizing the social façade. But we have to be rooted in what feeds our soul—the intimate knowledge of God—that the sweet meat within may grow and be there to feed the hungry. Aaron's rod is worth thinking about and taking to heart, in order that it might inform our actions.

Notes

INTRODUCTION

1. Tilden Edwards, et al., director of Shalem Institute in Washington, D.C., describes similar skewing in a research project in the mid-70s. See *Spiritual Growth: An Empirical Exploration of Its Meaning, Sources, and Implications* (Washington, D. C.: Alban Institute, 1974).
2. Urban T. Holmes, III, *A History of Christian Spirituality* (New York: Seabury, 1980; repr., Harrisburg, Pa.: Morehouse Publishing, 2002).

CHAPTER 1

1. Teresa of Avila, *The Interior Castle* (trans. Kieran Kavanaugh, O.C.D., and Otilio Rodriguez, O.C.D.), IV, 4.
2. David Bohm, *Wholeness and the Implicate Order* (London: Routledge & Kegan Paul, 1980).
3. Ignatius Loyola, *Spiritual Exercises* (trans. Louis J. Puhl, S.J.), 230–231.
4. Richard of St. Victor, *The Mystical Ark* (trans. Grover A. Zinn), I, 4.

CHAPTER 2

1. Urban T. Holmes, III, *The Priest in Community* (New York: Seabury, 1978).
2. William Willimon, *Worship and Pastoral Care* (Nashville, Tenn.: Abingdon, 1978).
3. Henri Nouwen, *The Wounded Healer* (Garden City, N.Y.: Doubleday, 1972).
4. Urban T. Holmes, III, *The Future Shape of Ministry* (New York: Seabury, 1971).

5. *The Cloud of Unknowing* (trans. Clifton Wolters), 14.
6. Sandra L. Bem, "The Measurement of Psychological Androgyny," *Journal of Counseling and Clinical Psychology.* XLII, 2 (1974): 161.
7. Ibid.
8. Ralph W. Hood, Jr., and James R. Hall, "Gender Differences in the Description of Erotic and Mystical Experiences," *Review of Religious Research*, XXI, 2 (1980): 195–207.

CHAPTER 3
1. Symeon the New Theologian, *Discourses* (trans. C. J. de Catanzaro), XII, 5.
2. Gregory of Nyssa, *The Life of Moses* (trans. Abraham I. Malherbe and Everett Ferguson), II, 59.
3. Nancy Van Scoyoc, *Women, Change, and the Church* (Nashville, Tenn.: Abingdon, 1980).
4. Gregory of Nyssa, *The Life of Moses*, II, 45.

CHAPTER 4
1. Richard of St. Victor, *The Mystical Ark* (trans. Grover A. Zinn), I, 4.
2. H. A. Williams, *True Christianity: The Oxford-Cambridge Lectures* (Springfield, Ill.: Templegate, 1975), p. 83.
3. Julian of Norwich, *Showings* [Long Text] (trans. Edmund Colledge, O.S.A., and James Walsh, S.J.), 46.
4. Henri Nouwen, *Reaching Out* (Garden City, N. Y.: Doubleday, 1975).
5. Julian of Norwich, *Showings* [Long Text], 46.

CHAPTER 5
1. Lewis Mumford, *The City in History* (New York: Harcourt, Brace, 1968).
2. H. A. Williams, *True Christianity: The Oxford-Cambridge Lectures* (Springfield, Ill.: Templegate, 1975), p. 38.
3. *The Global 2000 Report to the President* (Washington: U. S. Government Printing Office, 1980), vol. I, pp. 1–4.
4. H. A. Williams, *True Christianity*, pp. 40, 42.
5. Tilden Edwards, *Living Simply Through the Day* (New York: Paulist Press, 1977).
6. Edward M. Hays, *Secular Sanctity* (New York: Paulist Press, 1980), p. 67.

7. T. S. Eliot, *Murder in the Cathedral* (New York: Harcourt, Brace, 1935), p. 44.

CHAPTER 6
1. H. A. Williams, *True Christianity: The Oxford-Cambridge Lectures* (Springfield, Ill.: Templegate, 1975), p. 65.
2. Thomas Merton, *Emblems of a Season of Fury* (New York: New Directions, 1961), pp. 61, 63, 65, 67, 68.
3. Gregory of Nyssa, *The Life of Moses* (trans. Abraham J. Malherbe and Everett Ferguson), 11, 239.
4. Ibid., II, 282.
5. Teresa of Avila, *The Interior Castle* (trans. Kieran Kavanaugh, O.C.D. and Otilio Rodriguez, O.C.D.), VI, iv, 1–3.
6. Pierre Teilhard de Chardin, "The Evolution of Chastity" in *Toward the Future*, trans. René Hague (New York: Harcourt Brace Jovanovich, 1975). p. 77.
7. Ibid., p. 84.
8. Ibid., p. 72, emphasis author's.
9. "An Interview with Thomas Merton," *Motive*, XXVII (October, 1967): 37.
10. Nancy Van Scoyoc, *Women, Change, and the Church* (Nashville, Tenn.: Abingdon, 1980).

CHAPTER 7
1. Hadewijch, *Visions* (trans. Mother Columba Hart, O.S.B.), I, 288.
2. Ibid., VII, 64.
3. Thomas à Kempis, *The Imitation of Christ*, III, xiii, 1.
4. Louis Bouyer, *Liturgical Piety* (Notre Dame, Ind.: University of Notre Dame Press, 1945), p. 249.
5. Johann Arndt, *True Christianity* (trans. Peter Erb), V, ii, 9.
6. Ibid., V, ii, 12.
7. Gregory of Nyssa, *The Life of Moses* (trans. Abraham J. Malherbe and Everett Ferguson), II, 106.
8. John Donne, "Elegy on Mistris Boulstred."
9. George Herbert, "Death."
10. Ibid.
11. Ibid.
12. Bonaventure, *The Life of St. Francis* (trans Ewert Cousins), XIV, 1.
13. Julian of Norwich, *Showings* [Long Text] (trans. Edmund Colledge, O.S.A., and James Walsh, S.J.), 55.

CHAPTER 8

1. Julian of Norwich, *Showings* [Long Text] (trans. Edmund Colledge, O.S.A., and James Walsh, S.J.), 56.
2. Edward Edinger, *Ego and Archetype: Individuation and the Religious Function of the Psyche* (New York: Putnam, 1972), p. 109.
3. Gregory of Nyssa, *The Life of Moses* (trans. Abraham J. Malherbe and Everett Ferguson), II, 291.
4. Teresa of Avila, *The Interior Castle* (trans. Kieran Kavanaugh, O.C.D., and Otilio Rodriguez, O.C.D.), I, ii, 15.
5. Bonaventure, *The Tree of Life*, (trans. Ewert Cousins), Prologue, 1.
6. *The Cloud of Unknowing* (trans. Clifton Wolters), 7, 12.
7. John A. Sanford, *Healing and Wholeness* (New York: Paulist Press, 1977), p. 16.
8. Richard of St. Victor, *The Twelve Patriarchs* (trans. Grover A. Zinn), LXXI.
9. Teresa of Avila, *The Interior Castle*, I, ii, 9.

CHAPTER 9

1. John Harris, *Stress, Power, and Ministry* (Washington, D. C.: Alban Institute, 1977).
2. Athanasius, *The Life of Antony* (trans. Robert C. Gregg), 7.
3. William Law, *A Serious Call to a Devout and Holy Life*, 18.
4. Athanasius, *The Life of Antony* (trans. Robert C. Gregg), 14.
5. Henri Nouwen, *Reaching Out* (Garden City, N. Y.: Doubleday, 1975), p. 96.
6. Teresa of Avila, *The Interior Castle* (trans. Kieran Kavanaugh, O.C.D., and Otilio Rodriguez, O.C.D.), I, ii, 7.

CHAPTER 10

1. Sheldon Kopp, *The Hanged Man: Psychotherapy and the Forces of Darkness* (Palo Alto, Calif.: Science and Behavior Books, 1974), pp. 117–118.
2. Urban T. Holmes, III, *Ministry and Imagination* (New York: Seabury, 1976).
3. James Fenhagen, *More Than Wanderers* (New York: Seabury, 1978).
4. Gregory of Nyssa, *The Life of Moses* (trans. Abraham J. Malherbe and Everett Ferguson), II, 285.

Index

Aaron's rod, 177
Abandonment, by God, 115, 116
Accidie, 35
Accountability, 174–176
Acedia, 35, 36, 39, 46
Action, 110. *See also* Prayer
Adoration, 16
Affective style, xi, 88
Affluent pastors, 69–70
Agapē, 90, 93
Agenitive images, 31–32
Aelred of Rievaulx, 170–171
Allassō, 81
Allegorical interpretation, 124
Alter Christus, 26
American colonies, 22, 105
Anagogical interpretation, 124
Analytical modes, 7–8, 89
Anamnesis, 108
Androgyny, xi, 31–32, 91
Angels, 49
Anger, 41, 43, 175
Anglicans, ix, 68, 110, 121. *See also* Episcopalians
Animus, 130
Answer to Job (Jung), 125–126

Antiochus Epiphanes, 86
Antony of Egypt, 24, 145, 147
Apatheia, 86, 147
Apophatic style, xi, 14–15, 62, 79, 134–135, 176–177
Aristotelianism, 20
Aristotle, 6
Arndt, Johann, 105, 141
Ascetical theology, 20–21
Askēsis, 20, 30
Athanasius, 145, 147
Augustine of Hippo, 78–79, 86–87
Auricular learning, 156
Authentēo, 38
Awareness, new, 9–10, 11, 159, 175–176;
    instrument of, 33;
    and poverty, 71, 75, 79, 80;
    and unconscious, 122

Baptism, 105, 108, 109, 112, 113–116
Baptists, 37
Beatitudes, 68
Beatrice, 60
Beghards, 103

183

Wagon masters, 174
Wandering preachers, colonial
   American, 22
Warm sins, 36
Water resources, 75
Weil, Simone, 23
*Wholeness and the Implicate
   Order* (Bohm), 9
Will, 66
William of St. Thierry, 109
Williams, Charles, 152
Williams, H. A., 56, 58, 71, 74,
   85
Williams, Tennessee, 36
Willimon, William, 25
Witches, 151
Wittgenstein, Ludwig, 8
Wolf children, 6–7

Women: and sexual issues,
   93–94, 98
in study, xi, 57
   See also Femininity
Women, Change, and the Church
   (Van Scoyoc), 45, 98
Worldviews, x–xi
   canonic, xi, 128
   charismatic, xi, 128, 168
   empiric, xi, 128, 164, 168
   gnostic, xi, 61, 164
World View Study, x–xi, 164
Worship, 103–119, 121
   See also Liturgy
Worship and Pastoral Care
   (Willimon), 25
Wounded Healer (Nouwen), 25
Zwingli, H., 111